The Love of God

Is Anyone There?

Robe

Welcome

In these pages I have shared something of myself.
It's the best I can offer so far.
I'd be glad to hear your story too.

tamariskbooks@yahoo.co.uk

or care of
info@opaltrust.org

Published by: Tamarisk Publications, Chester, United Kingdom
Email: tamariskbooks@yahoo.co.uk

Produced for Tamarisk Publications by Dolman Scott
  <www.dolmanscott.com>
Printed in the United Kingdom.

Distributed by: Opal Trust, 1 Glenannan Park, Lockerbie DG11 2FA,
  Scotland, United Kingdom
Phone / fax (UK): 01576 203670
Email: info@opaltrust.org
Web: www.opaltrust.org

* * * * * * * * * * *

Thanks, as always, to my near and dear – to Janet for proof-reading and to Becky for the illustrations. Special thanks to Elise Gibson, Doug Moffat and Paul Dann for many perceptive insights and suggestions. Also to Chris Mellor and Colin Randall for helpful comments and encouragement. You have made me think!

Questions for thought and discussion are at the back of the book. Bible references, identified with numerals, are shown at the foot of each page. Other references, indicated by letters, are listed in the endnotes.

The Love of God
Is Anyone There?

TO KNOW HIM

It is a strange and perhaps a universal experience that when things go really well, people who normally have no interest in God will feel profoundly thankful. We may not know who to thank, or how to express thanks, and yet are undeniably thankful.

And when things go wrong, people with no religious commitment will speak as though God is somehow involved.

He enters our personal consciousness when things happen that we have not planned and cannot control. Most of the time we keep him out, but then for a brief instant we count him in.

Why is this? Could it be that we really know more than we claim to believe? Do we understand more than we think?

Here We Are

For each of us there are moments when we wonder about God. Such a feeling may quickly pass and leave no trace. Or it may raise a flag suggesting something to think about when time allows. It may awaken a definite desire to know the truth. It may even mark the first step in an urgent quest that will not rest until fully satisfied.

Belief in God is a personal thing. We do not like to trespass on the holy ground of another person's faith. We may not find it easy to talk about our own. At the same time, a friend who is willing to be vulnerable and speak shyly of their trust in God may touch our heart and bring great comfort when we need it most.

Our beliefs make us the people we are, affecting all we say and do – our priorities, our attitudes and responses. We have serious questions about life and death, and especially about God. Does he exist, and if he does, what is he like? Does he care about us, and if so can we make contact with him?

Often we are afraid to ask someone who might know. The culture we live in does not encourage us to talk about these things. There seems to be a conspiracy of silence. Yet all around are people who believe in him and draw great strength from their belief. Surely they would welcome our interest. They might even become our closest friends.

Some of us come from families with no spiritual awareness, and we simply wonder if there is something we are missing.

Others have always had a feeling that there is a spiritual side to life, mysterious and difficult to define.

Some have made a significant mark on the world with career, family and public responsibilities, then in retirement have more time to think about the meaning and purpose of it all.

But an interest in God is by no means limited to a few who are curious to know if he exists. Questions are raised by others in most unlikely places.

Some have attended church services all their life, and yet admit that God still seems obscure and difficult to trace. If we are honest, an invisible spirit is hard to know and harder still to love.

Others with intellectual issues never found anyone willing or able to discuss them. Questions have gone unanswered, doubts fester without resolution. Weary of pretence, you drift into unbelief.

Some have personal failures or past hurts severely undermining their trust in God. He is no longer involved in the things that matter most. Faith becomes divorced from life and provides little help or comfort.

Others have become disillusioned with organised religion, bearing the scars perhaps of unhappy experience – spiritual hype and manipulation, illusive signs and wonders, or miracles that never happened.

Some of us used to go to church but now feel more aware of God in the garden or by the sea than among the chairs or pews. Yet we do not want to lose our faith completely, nor to leave our children ignorant of what may still be true.

Then of course there are the ordinary people who would not think of going to church but still have some faith in something. Believing the little you know, you would be quite willing to find out more. In fact, now that we have invited you, you will cheerfully join us in our quest.

Here we are then, a group of friends – different in many ways – and yet with something of great interest in common. We would like to know what can be known about the God who is, we think, somewhere not far away.

But life is not easy. We need a faith that will give us strength to cope with the circumstances we are in. Too often we feel restless and unhappy. We might wonder: If God is there, is he willing to give us any help?

Why Am I So Restless?

We live in an unsettled world. All around us people are uneasy and dissatisfied. We know what it feels like. We search constantly for something to make us feel better, pinning our hopes on an exotic holiday or a new hairstyle or cosmetic surgery or fashion clothes or a gym subscription or sports club. Continually shifting things around, we alter kitchens and bathrooms, change jobs, upgrade equipment, swap cars, move house, leave one partner for another.

Nothing is ever quite right because we're too uneasy to be settled in anything for long. Restlessly we tweet and text, surf the web, channel-hop TV. We fidget and fuss, take shopping trips and buy things we do not want. We joke and flirt, pick a quarrel, start an affair, drink to excess and remain still empty and unsatisfied. We are hungry for something but cannot tell what it may be.

Then we see it in others, and even in ourselves – a craving for attention, admiration, flattery and power. For some it becomes an obsession with business, profit and career, forbidding even a moment's relaxation. For others it shows itself in constant criticisms and complaints. Finally it shouts its unhappiness in road rage, arguments at home, disputes between neighbours, quarrels over credit and debt, prosecutions, claims, libels and more subtle defamations of character.

Someone has said, "Three quarters of the ill-nature of the world is caused by the fact that the soul without God is empty and so out of rest."[a] As Augustine long ago observed in his prayer to his maker, "You made us for yourself, and our hearts find no peace until they rest in you."[b]

Here then is our starting point. You have some honest belief in God, though perhaps much less than you might wish. You have some interest in the Bible, although parts of it may seem hard to accept or understand. You have a genuine respect for Jesus, whilst feeling you may have failed him in some way. But above all, you are hungry, restless and dissatisfied. Be reassured that you are not alone; you are among friends.

1.

Setting Out Together

Restless and dissatisfied, something essential is missing from my life. If God is a possibility, I need to know whatever can be known of him. If he is good and loving, as many believe, there would be everything to gain from making contact with him. If he is wanting to help us where we are, we really need some help. If he exists it would be much better to live with him than without him… or even perhaps against him.

We need reliable information. Science, history and careful thought must all have a part to play in this most extraordinary quest for evidence of God. Wherever he may be, or whatever he may be like, our concern is to know the truth. We must use any means we can to discover it.

Some might see this as a spiritual journey. Pressing on through the mist that obscures every spiritual path, we will keep a lookout for landmarks as we go – things we can be sure of while continuing to explore areas of uncertainty. Gradually we must establish what we can firmly accept and depend upon.

Feelings at this point are probably quite mixed – a measure of discontent that our destination seems so far off, yet undeniable excitement that we are finally on our way. After a first step there should be definite progress, with happy discoveries along the road, some poignant moments, and perhaps some unexpected surprises.

Encouragement we shall certainly find in the Bible, for in its pages we will meet many people on the same road, and some who have travelled far. "When we read about the great men and women of the scriptures, it is not so much their courage or even the power of their exploits that grips us. Rather, the intimacy with which they walked with God stirs within us a passion to know him as they knew him."[c]

Then in due course we will try speaking in words to God himself, hoping he might hear us and respond. The Bible says, "Draw near to God, and he will draw near to you."[1] We will attempt this and see what happens.

Certainly we are a mixed company, and different in many ways from the world around us. Some of us embarked on this quest long ago and are still searching. Others are setting out this very day. Some have no religious roots and would like to investigate the possibility of God. Others used to believe but lost touch somewhere along the way. Some have set out with keen energy and expectation. Others pursue their course with a measure of wistfulness, increasingly faint and erratic as the years go by. Some are dissatisfied, perhaps sadly discouraged, seeing small signs of spiritual reality. A few may even have lost hope and are near to giving up. Speaking honestly, we will learn to love and trust and support one another. Hard questions and personal challenges must be faced if we intend to uncover all the truth, but we will face these together, without fear or shame, helping one another along the way.

A Sense of Wonder

To start with, we need some clear evidence we can depend on. It may be nearer to us than we think. If a seagull in flight were not so common we would stand amazed and watch it soar. If the world contained a single daisy we would gaze astonished at its beauty. If the night sky were suddenly for the first time revealed to human sight, we would be overwhelmed by its glorious immensity. As it is, we are too often blind to the marvel of familiar things.

If we could stop the car as the sun sinks behind the distant mountains, we might come to see our problems in a very different light. If there were only time to linger at the lakeside and hear the wind in the reeds, we might sense a presence profoundly comforting and calm. If we could just pause among the butterflies in a sunny woodland clearing, we might enjoy a brief foretaste of paradise.

---

[1] James 4:8

As it is, we are always busy – too busy to stop, too busy to become aware. Day by day, year by year, we do what is expected. Duty calls and demands our full attention. The working day passes quickly, and commercial entertainments exhaust our leisure hours.

One writer claims, "Wonder is the prelude to knowledge."[d] He is right. And if we do not yet know anything about God, it may be that we have lost (or never had) a sense of wonder. What we lack is not a faith to believe but a moment to marvel and half an hour to think.

The first step in our quest is not a step at all but a choice to sit still for a little while and observe. "Awareness of the divine begins with wonder."[e] Pause to look closely at the natural world and you may be moved to whisper, "This is the LORD's doing and it is marvellous in our eyes."[1]

But wonder, on its own, will not take us far. You may vaguely wonder all your life and never grasp the significance of a single thing. For many of us indeed, the needed stimulus to search and find comes through discontent. It is our restlessness that moves us on.

Human discoveries are generally made by people unhappy with the way things are. Weary of stress and conflict, disillusioned with the bustle, the noise and the old routine – sorrowful perhaps, alienated and misunderstood, longing for reality and almost ready to despair – at this very point of weakness and humiliation, I realize there must be a better way to live. Suddenly I am resolved to find it.

If awareness begins with wonder, and searching follows from discontent, then knowledge grows through careful enquiry. With an open heart and an open mind, we must sift the evidence for clear facts we can depend upon. Taking nothing for granted, ignoring all that is commonly believed and accepted, we must decide for ourselves what we can personally accept and believe.

First Thoughts

With an honest mind and a humble heart, we are heading out in search of God, looking for clues, seeking for traces of his presence wherever they may be found.

Few people are unmoved by the glory, the majesty, the intricate detail of the natural world. The oxygen factory silently at work in

---

[1] Psalm 118:23

every leaf, the remarkable properties of water, the strange enigma of electricity, the glowing light of a firefly, the adhesive properties of an insect's feet, the unseen potential in an acorn, the formation of a butterfly from the residue of a caterpillar – these are the so-called marvels of Nature. But you yourself are more marvellous than any of them. The human ear, the human eye, the lungs and heart and brain and reproductive system: study these carefully and you will never again take yourself for granted.

It seems highly unlikely that such fantastic machines could have fallen into place by chance. We do not see it happening today and have no proof that it happened in the past. Wherever complex mechanisms are found, a creative intelligence has been at work – conscious, intentional and capable. In our experience, design is always evidence of designer.

Who was it, then, that devised the molecular structures? Who conceived the electrical impulses and chemical reactions of the nervous system? Who wrote the genetic codes determining the shape and function of every living thing? If there is a program, there must surely have been a programmer. If there is writing, there must have been a writer. Evidence of design in us and in the world around us is too consistent and too abundant for an open-minded person to deny the probability of an intelligent architect and engineer.

In fact, no *human* invention gives us anything like the same sense of awe and delight as the universe we live in, for no human invention is as vast or as tiny, and none is so exquisite. The natural world is both functional and beautiful, and the closer we look, the more complex the functions appear, and the more astonishing the beauty. The laws and processes underlying all of science point to an architect of awesome imaginative intelligence, a creator whose universe extends in light-years beyond human measurement and yet attends to details so small that our instruments cannot yet distinguish them. And in all this he reveals himself as a visionary artist and a lover of loveliness.

But once we suppose that there is a designer we urgently need to know more about him. Can we discover anything definite about his character and his intentions? Is he still involved in caring for his creation? If this astonishing universe has a maker, where is he? What is he like? Can we actually make contact with him? Then at a more personal level: Is he aware of me? Does he care at all about me? Is he wanting to help me in any way?

In general we receive confused or uncertain answers to such questions, leaving us year after year perplexed and undecided. We may even give up asking, until honesty insists on raising the same question again. Does anyone know for sure? Can we discover the truth about the creator of the universe? What evidence is there?

From Where I Am

We often make this harder than it needs to be, by looking in the wrong place. You will find the most accessible traces of your maker not in the sky or in a church or in a book but in yourself! Examine more carefully what you are like and you will understand a great deal about your designer.

If there is a God, and if he made the world, then you are certainly the finest thing in his creation. He could think of nothing better to make than a human being. Here we have some definite information about him. He is the sort of person who would choose to invent you.

Every engineer will value the capabilities he gives to his greatest and most complex invention. The machine can do what it does because he knew in his own mind what it would do if he made it that way. In this sense it is an expression of his own personality and purpose. It does what he himself would like to do if he were where it is.

But while a single invention may perform one task well, the inventor is capable of far more. He can choose the shape and size of his invention, decide exactly how it works, adapt it for varied circumstances, repair the machine if it goes wrong, and make many other inventions too. Does this, we might wonder, provide us with any clues to the character of God?

Firstly, if he has made us, we would expect him to have capabilities far exceeding ours. But secondly, if we are indeed his finest invention, we would expect him to have a personality and purpose similar to our own. We can do what he would like to do if he were in our place.

The earliest of the Bible writers came to exactly this conclusion and none of them found any reason to dispute it. They saw evidence that "God created man *in his own image*."[1] In other words, God created us *to be like himself*. He made us capable of doing what he does.

---

[1] Genesis 1:27

But are we simply looking at ourselves and imagining there is a god like us? Of course, that is exactly what we would do if we were made like him. But it does not mean he is just imaginary. We can imagine something we have never seen and then find it is exactly what we imagined it to be.

This is very helpful. It means that you can learn a great deal about God from what you know of yourself. If you can see and hear, it seems likely that he too can see and hear. If you can think and remember, so too can he. If you have a desire to speak and communicate, so does he. If you can plan for the future, so can he. If you feel happy and sad, so does he. If you enjoy some things and dislike some things, so indeed does he. And what is more, if his capabilities exceed ours, he can do all these things far better than we can.

Yet looking more closely at ourselves we may not be quite so pleased with what we find. We may even have reason to hope that God is not like us at all.

Second Thoughts

Not like us at all: why is that? The world around us is both astonishingly wonderful and deeply perplexing. To study it with an open mind is to be convinced there is an intelligence behind it all, and indeed a good and benevolent intelligence. Every biological organ is perfect in form and function, intricately conceived to fulfil its necessary role. Every physical process plays its essential part in the fantastic machine we call planet earth. Creation itself has been lovingly conceived and constructed.

But then we look more closely and receive a terrible shock. Every living thing is damaged in some way. We see beautiful creatures suffering horrible diseases, tranquil oceans swept by tsunami waves, peaceful cities destroyed by earthquakes, farmland scarred by floods and fires, populations wiped out by famines and plagues. And in the end every living thing, so wonderfully made, grows old and feeble, endures illness and disease, then finally and inevitably dies.

An onlooker might suppose a vandal has been at work, and this may not be far from the truth. Creation, so perfect in design and construction, has been wrecked, disfigured and left in disarray. Good and evil did not co-operate in creation. The evidence we have shows that good came first and was later corrupted by evil. We do not see a bad design anywhere, but we see every good design menaced in some way by something or someone th distresses and despoils it. Who has done this? There seem to bu powers of evil at loose in this world – enemies to all that is good, aliens who played no part in its original design, rebel forces in opposition to its maker.

As human beings we suffer as much, and perhaps far more, than any other creature. Every organ in our body is vulnerable to damage, disease, degeneration and ultimately death. At birth we are like a brand new car, bright and shining as it leaves the factory, but then it develops mechanical faults, suffers bumps and scratches, succumbs to rust, and finally ends up as scrap. Or like a beautiful house, planned and built with exquisite care and skill, whose foundations are then washed away, its beams infected with dry rot, its windows broken and its fittings looted. Before long, without repair, the house will collapse and fall. That is what we are like, beautifully designed but now in a tragic state of disrepair.

But the problem runs deeper than this. It touches our personality, our heart and mind and secret motivations. Every member of the human race is both awesome and embarrassing. We know this from our own experience. We simply do not live up to our expectations.

We have ideals but fail to follow them. We make promises but do not keep them. We know what is right and yet do wrong. We long to be proud of our achievements but then tell lies to cover our shame. We have done things we would much rather forget. We have caused trouble to ourselves and to others. This is our human predicament – we are familiar with it – but what can it teach us about our maker? Out of all this human chaos, can we learn anything definite about God?

Our Highest Ideals

From the stones that remain, an archaeologist can tell you much about a building that has long since tumbled down. Even the wreck of a car may be identified by colour and by make, and its value at the time of impact ascertained. Every ruin reveals something of its former glory and offers clues to the character of its architect and builder.

Granted that the image of God in us has been spoiled and marred, there should be clues amidst the wreckage revealing something about us and about our maker too. Despite the human damage that we have suffered in body and in mind, we would expect to find some traces of his personality in us still. But how can we identify those traces and reconstruct what once was there?

On rare occasions you are moved to behave better than you ever learned from your parents or your school or church. Occasionally you will surprise yourself by being more patient or more generous than you thought possible. You do something good and considerate when nobody is watching and no one will ever find out. Then you are compelled to conclude: This is not me, this is God in me.

In what you know to be your best moments you come closest to discerning the character of God. More often we wish we had been better than we were. At the same time there are people we meet whose kindness and helpfulness – far beyond the call of duty – leave us humbled and amazed; we distinctly see something of God in them.

Where does this take us? If we gather up all we admire in people we know, and the very best of our own highest ideals – ignoring all we dislike in others and ourselves – it is possible to picture the kind of people we were meant to be and so recover a certain knowledge of our maker. There is much to be discerned in this way but it is intensely personal. Nobody can prove it to you; it is something you find out for yourself. For some people it is immediately obvious; for others it will take more effort, more time and more consideration.

The Evidence We Have

What progress have we made so far in our quest for the truth about God? In our quieter moments we have sensed the peace that passes understanding. Design we have observed in the natural world. Traces of glory we have identified in our own humanity. But there is far more evidence than that, and we must study it carefully.

What exactly is said, for example, in that amazing anthology of miscellaneous writings we call the Bible? This remarkable book was compiled by forty or more authors, separated by oceans, mountains and deserts during a period of sixteen hundred years. But their contrasting circumstances and experiences convinced them all of one thing – that the creator of this world cares about his creation and wants to communicate with it. They claimed to have personal experience of this. We will see what we can learn from them.

Many people would say the most interesting character in the Bible is Jesus Christ. He was known, of course, as a great teacher, and often spoke about the *love* of God. He devoted his life to helping people with problems, and those who knew him best believed they saw the character of God in him more clearly than in any other human being. They wrote a careful record of what happened in those days, and we will take a close look at it.

Heading into the unknown is, for anyone, a risky venture: we must take care how we go. The signposts we have found so far give some assurance we may be on the right track. If so, we should expect more confirmation in the stages that lie ahead. Indeed, the nearer we get to our goal the clearer it should become.

2.

A Little Knowledge

Many people, perhaps most people, have a quiet belief in God. It is often a strong belief but extremely vague in detail. As such it would be a firm faith in an unknown god, and one who perhaps cannot be known. But along with this, there is often a secret desire to know him.

Maybe for this reason, paperbacks will sell in large numbers bearing a title such as *Knowing God,* or *The Knowledge of the Holy,* or *Knowing the Face of God.* The reader may buy and open such a book with high expectations and yet some weeks later admit with regret that it has failed to satisfy. We still do not really know God.

Perhaps the title was misleading, promising more than any author can supply. In reality the face of God has never been glimpsed, except for a few brief years when the people of Galilee and Judea believed they saw "the glory of God in the face of Jesus Christ".[1] A knowledge of the Holy is surely beyond the reach of earthly imperfection. And knowing God in any practical sense seems quite impossible when he is invisible, and presumably infinite and eternal, and moves in realms inaccessible to humankind.

We must be honest. To know God as I know my children or my friends or my wife is quite beyond me. On this earth, Jesus alone has claimed in truth to know God. "I know him," he said, "for I

---

[1] 2 Corinthians 4:6

come from him, and he sent me."[1] Neither Moses, nor Job, nor Paul, nor any other Bible writer claimed this. As for us, our hearts and minds remain clouded by our humanity and our ungodliness. We are not heavenly but earthly people. Are we then to despair of really knowing him? Must we abandon all thought of knowing him even a little?

Someone has said that a little knowledge is a dangerous thing. But a little knowledge only becomes dangerous when misused. A little knowledge of God would surely be a wonderful thing. Unable to fathom the vast expanse of the universe, we still appreciate the beauty of the stars. Unfamiliar with the ocean depths, we still enjoy the breaking waves. To know him a little would be far better than not knowing him at all.

An awareness of the living God is always tinged with wonder, wistfulness and awe. A genuine encounter has usually left a man or woman humbled and sometimes unnerved and seriously shaken. In fact the more we know of him, the more we feel our ignorance. It has been said, "Look, these are just the outskirts of his ways, and how small a whisper do we hear of him! Who then can understand the thunder of his power?"[2]

And yet a little knowledge is far more satisfying than none. Indeed, for the time being, it may be all we need. I do not understand exactly how my car works, but I know enough to drive it safely. I cannot tell how a radio picks up airwaves but I know enough to find a station I would like to hear.

The little we do know will often hint at further possibilities consistent with that knowledge. Finding out when my great-grandfather was born and married and had children, I will expect other details of his life to be consistent with those facts. And knowing a little about something or someone may give us a deep affection for what we know. Although ignorant of many things concerning my hometown, my language and even my own family I know enough to love them, to appreciate them, and to be confident of learning more.

All this suggests that the little we know of God is valuable and could well increase. Slowly, or perhaps suddenly, I become aware of him. At first, like a small child introduced to an uncle I have never met, I feel shy and insecure. Hardly daring to raise my eyes, I wait for him to speak. But he has a welcoming smile and a kind

[1] John 7:29
[2] Job 26:14

voice; he seems friendly. Gently he puts me at ease, taking an interest in my doings. He tells me about himself, winning my confidence and then my affection. Before long I am willing to speak up for him, and even to suffer scorn and mockery for his sake. Eventually I am happy to declare, "I am not ashamed, for *I know whom I have believed.*"[1] So we may progress from shyness at first, through warm confidence, to fierce loyalty, "increasing in the knowledge of God."[2] We encourage one another, "Let us know; let us press on to know the LORD."[3]

You will never know everything about the creator of the universe, and yet you may know some things about him that are true. If they are true, you can depend upon them with your life.

If, on the other hand, I ignore what can be known of him, the fault is surely mine. Indeed we are justly warned, "Some have no knowledge of God. I say this to your shame."[4]

Seeking and Finding

In our search for the living God we will certainly attempt our honest best, but how far is that likely to take us? What if God himself does not wish to be found? What if he has no need of us, or no desire for us? If he resolved to remain hidden he could surely do so and all our efforts would be in vain. Do we have any reason to suppose he will help us in our quest? Does he wish to communicate with us at all?

For several thousand years people have asked this question and consistently reached the same conclusion. After all, in the stillness of evening it is not a remote or unfriendly being whose presence comforts and uplifts. In troublesome circumstances it is not an inscrutable and uncommunicative deity who inspires a gentler and kinder approach to life.

There are many ways of communicating. The whole of creation proclaims the glory of God. Jesus himself was always talking, explaining, answering, teaching. And a sensitive conscience which speaks for God in each of us will say as much as we will let him say. When we are most receptive to his revelation, he is a God who reveals himself. He communicates. He responds to those who seek him.

---

[1] 2 Timothy 1:12
[2] Colossians 1:10
[3] Hosea 6:3
[4] 1 Corinthians 15:34

The Bible writers did not think it foolish to go in search of God. "Seek the LORD and his strength," they said, "seek his presence continually!"[1] Indeed as a matter of urgency we should seek him lest the opportunity be lost. "Seek the LORD while he may be found," they said, "and call upon him while he is near."[2] What surprised them more was the realisation that he himself is watching and waiting for us to make a move: "God looks down from heaven on the children of mankind to see if there are any who understand, who seek after God."[3]

Then one of the Bible writers became convinced of something even more unexpected. Looking at the history of tribes and nations in the world, he found good reason to believe that God "fixed beforehand the exact times and limits of the places where they lived." And there was a specific reason for this, "so they would *seek God*, and perhaps feel their way towards him and find him, although he is not far from every one of us."[4]

Our own experience surely bears this out. In every nation we see people restless and disillusioned with the way things are. Unsettled where we live, unhappy with our generation, dissatisfied with our limits of time and place, we look for something beyond what we can see and hear and touch. It is our frustration with the world we know that leads us to seek for something higher and better, to grope and stumble as best we can towards whoever or whatever may be there. But are we then doomed to seek forever, restlessly, hopelessly and without success? Or have our circumstances been planned by God *with this specific purpose* – that we might seek him and find him and so come to rest?

If that is the case, then our greatest tragedy would be to seek him all our life and *never* finally track him down. It is imperative that we find him. Indeed, our personal safety depends upon it. Drowning in a lake, you struggle for a breath of air, and if you cannot take it you will die. Bitten by a snake, you race to find some antidote and if you do not get it you will die. So the Bible writers urge us, "Seek the Lord and live."[5]

Experience led them to believe that whoever truly seeks him will find him. Moses was so certain of this that he could promise his people, "You will seek the LORD your God and *you will find him,*

---

[1] 1 Chronicles 16:11
[2] Isaiah 55:6
[3] Psalm 53:2
[4] Acts 17:26-27
[5] Amos 5:6

if you search for him with all your heart and with all your soul."[1]
Jesus was so sure of it that he promised his followers, "Seek, and
you will find; knock, and it will be opened to you."[2]

All this gives us no reason for despair and much cause for hope.
Indeed, if I am truly seeking him, I can be sure to find him seeking
me. A good shepherd will go looking for a lost lamb. In the end it
is found, not because the lamb knew the way but because the
shepherd knew the way.

We have strong grounds to believe that God exists, that he wants
us to seek him, and indeed that he strongly desires us to find him.
But how, in practical terms, will he help us in our quest?

Beyond our Reach

On a cloudy day you may put on hiking boots and head up a
valley, not knowing exactly what lies ahead. Climbing steadily you
sense there are mountains all around, but so covered in mist that no
one can tell where they might be or how high they are. Later the
weather clears a little and you begin to glimpse the majestic
beauty, and also the steepness of the way. Many a spiritual journey
begins like this with enthusiasm but then starts to falter as
difficulties loom ahead.

Like the highest peak, the Most High God remains invisible,
always out of sight and out of reach. We cannot see or touch him.
We believe he is there but many things about him remain unclear.
What exactly is he like? How does he feel about human beings? Is
he angry with us? Does he like us? Are we a disappointment to
him? Would he prefer to forget about us altogether? Does he
perhaps feel sorry for us, or even want to help?

We would certainly appreciate some help. The spinning planet
we call home is troubled and disordered by terrible famines and
disasters, by incessant wars and epidemics. So neglected does it
appear that some might think it a God-forsaken place. Has its
maker simply abandoned the old machine to run down and
disintegrate with no attempt at maintenance or repair? Are we left
to suffer the consequences of our human ignorance and folly with
no help or comfort, no guidance or direction?

Imagine for a moment that you are the creator. You have
designed and made a world for people to live in. Like you, they can

---

[1] Deuteronomy 4:29
[2] Matthew 7:7

see and hear and think and remember; they have a creative intelligence like your own. In fact they are by far the best thing you ever made. But their world has gone wrong and they suffer pain and terrible distress.

Down there on the surface of the planet are millions of them, trying to make contact with you – talking to you, thanking you, offering gifts, asking for guidance and pleading for your help. Is it likely that, as an inventor, you would take no further interest in your best invention? Are you content for it to disintegrate and fail? If only for the sake of your reputation, you would surely wish to use your knowledge of its workings to attempt a permanent repair. And if, as those tiny humans have reason to believe, you are greater and better than they are, you will care about their world even more than they do and have compassion on their crying need.

But two enormous difficulties lie in your way. Firstly, the world is a single planet and the problems it faces are global in extent. Many of its inhabitants are not seeking to solve those problems but rather to make them worse, exploiting human weakness and promoting conflict for their own advantage. Given a choice, in fact, very few would prefer heaven to earth. Only a small minority would want to change the way things are if it meant giving up what they have.

How can you mend the machine when mankind in general prefers it the way it is and will not want your help? You might make a unilateral decision to halt all disease, decay and death. But if you did, the world's tyrants and dictators would simply remain in lusty health to exploit and oppress the rest of us for ever. The world cannot be put to rights until all its inhabitants want it put right. Only then will it stay right. But how could human nature, on a global scale, without exception, be so radically and completely changed?

Secondly and more immediately, there is a problem of affinity. You fill the heaven of heavens whilst they are minute human animals on the surface of the earth. How would you communicate with them? Their understanding and experience is so limited. You might awaken the conscience and imagination of some who are unusually sensitive. You might speak audibly to prophets, or appear in dreams and visions to seers. But there remains one enormous problem. You are an infinite spiritual being whilst they struggle to survive in a solid material world. Severely restricted by laws of gravity, energy, motion and mass, they cannot come to you. They can only beg you to come to them.

Many times indeed their heartfelt cry is for the Lord God to visit and redeem his people. And why should he not do such a thing? You could go and live among them, wear their clothes, visit their homes, talk with them in their language, help them with their problems, explain things of which they are entirely ignorant. You could prepare the world for a day when it might be mended and put right, and at the same time separate those who want it mended from those who do not.

If this is a possibility, no one should be so foolish as to reject it out of hand – especially as evidence exists to suggest it really happened. For a short while God became visible; he became human. He was born as a baby and grew up as a boy. People called him Jesus of Nazareth.

They also called him the Son of God. But why did they think of him in those terms?

The Embodiment of God

Jesus told his followers, "I have come down from heaven."[1] Now that is a very strange thing to say. Those are not the words of someone who was simply a good teacher or even a wonderful man. They are the words of someone who claimed to be a heavenly being. If a man says, "I have come down from heaven," there are three possibilities. He is either deliberately lying, or suffering a mental delusion, or telling the truth.

Nothing about Jesus would lead us to suppose he was a liar or a crackpot. Many people who knew him were convinced, and openly affirmed, "He is the image of the invisible God."[2] "In him," they said, "the whole fullness of deity dwells in bodily form."[3] They had no doubt about it. The infinite God really did become "incarnate"; he was "embodied", he became a man and lived on earth. But how does this help us?

It means that if we want to know what God is like, we can simply look at Jesus and enquire: What was Jesus like? And that is a question easily answered. We know exactly what he was like because those who knew him best have told us.

They shared a house with him, walked long roads with him, ate their meals with him, climbed hills and mountains with him. They went fishing with him, attended weddings, dinners and funerals

---

[1] John 6:38
[2] Colossians 1:15
[3] Colossians 2:9

with him. For a period of three years they spent all their days and nights with him. He spoke their language, met their families, saw their doubts and hesitations, heard their hopes and fears, helped them with their difficulties, and explained to them day by day things they did not know.

The world they lived in was as shocking and chaotic as it is today. People were as distressed and perplexed then as they are now. It was to Jesus they turned for information and advice. To him they appealed for rescue from dark occult powers. To him they cried for safety in time of mortal danger. To him they turned for help when no one else could do a thing.

He went from place to place putting right whatever had gone wrong – straightening bent limbs, restoring blind eyes, opening deaf ears, driving out evil spirits, enabling the severely paralysed to walk, teaching the ignorant, forgiving the guilty, transforming the corrupt, and even raising the dead to life. There was no problem he could not solve, no sorrow he could not relieve, no personal tragedy he could not reverse and overcome.

In every situation he knew exactly what to do. Peter at his wit's end confessed, "Master, we toiled all night and took nothing! *But at your word* I will let down the nets." In a crisis at a wedding his mother Mary simply told the stewards, *"Do whatever he tells you."* Those who knew him best had learned to trust him most completely.

What can we learn from this? If Jesus had added to the troubles of the world, or if he had been indifferent to them, we might suspect that our creator is unconcerned about our anxieties, our adversities and our most desperate needs. Yet Jesus committed himself to solving the kind of problems we all face. He was concerned, and able, and willing to put things right. That is the kind of God we need and, according to the evidence, the kind of God we have. Knowing what he can do, and did, our greatest wisdom will surely be to trust him with the doing of it, in his way and in his time.

When a complex machine breaks down, the person best qualified to mend it will be the one who designed and built it. With his extraordinary ability to repair human beings, Jesus could do what we would expect of a creator. That is the definite impression we have from those who wrote about him. But are their writings reliable? Is the evidence they offer entirely trustworthy? We must do some more research.

We are Witnesses

The four writers of the documents we call the Gospels were among the most intelligent people of their day. We can be certain of that. At a time when few were well-educated they had learned to write extremely well. What is more, they knew what they were writing about. Matthew was himself a disciple of Jesus and so was John. Mark probably wrote down what Peter told him and may also have been present on many of the occasions he recounts. Luke is concerned to tell us he recorded the testimony of reliable eyewitnesses.

All four took great care with details such as numbers, names, and places. There is no boastfulness or hype, no undue excitement or obvious exaggeration, nothing but a simple factual account of what was said and done. The incidents they describe had been witnessed by many people, and most of what they said was common knowledge. They clearly believed their report to be accurate and true.

So did their friends. Some took the trouble to copy out what they had written, every word, by hand. If their contemporaries had not confirmed what they said, the Gospel narratives would not have survived. If the second and subsequent generations had not been equally convinced, those pages would never have been preserved or further copies made.

These eyewitness accounts from Galilee and Judea bring us face to face with a most unusual person. To his generation Jesus was undoubtedly an enigma. At first his disciples were bewildered. And the more they discovered about him, the more bewildered they became. "What sort of man is this?" they asked.[1]

He was quite unlike anyone else. First there was the curious affirmation by both Mary and Joseph that their baby came from God without human intercourse. Then came his extraordinary ability to heal not just some diseases but any disease, at any time, with a simple word or a touch. He could ignore gravity, stop the wind, wither a fig tree, change water into wine, replace a severed ear and instantly multiply fish and bread. Crucified, dead and buried, he walked out of his tomb alive and well.

To say he was unique is an understatement. There had never been anyone remotely like him. In his personality the men and women around him saw absolute goodness, purity, unselfishness and

---

[1] Matthew 8:27

honesty. With no trace of human nature's darker side, he was at all times loving, compassionate, sensitive, inspiring and uplifting. By all accounts he was a perfect man. In fact the only fault anyone could find in him was this: "You being a man make yourself God."[1] And if that was the truth, how could it be a fault?

We should not suppose that people in those days were unduly gullible. Among them were many such as Thomas who refused to believe without convincing proof. Seeing it, they were then totally convinced. Jesus was a very public figure and everyone knew what he was doing. When his disciples recorded details of people and times and places, they were not passing on wild rumours or fanciful tales heard second- or third-hand about incidents far away. Peter said, "We are witnesses of all that he did."[2] John affirmed, "We have seen his glory."[3]

These men, declaring what had happened, would lay down their lives rather than deny the truth of it. Ordered to speak no more about Jesus, they insisted, "We cannot stop speaking of what we have seen and heard."[4] Several times they were arrested and imprisoned – one of them was put to death and another prepared for execution – but still they would not keep quiet. It was true and important, and must be made known.

Perhaps you doubt this talk of miracles. That is understandable. Be aware however that those present at the time were perfectly clear about it. They had seen what happened; they recorded it in detail and insisted on it at cost of liberty and life.

---

[1] John 10:33
[2] Acts 10:39
[3] John 1:14
[4] Acts 4:20

3.

The Son of God

In two ways Jesus has shown us the character of God – so his disciples believed – through his life and through his teaching. As we have seen, he lived among the people as God would live, doing the kind of things that God alone could do. But he also taught them directly about his heavenly Father. And it is clear that he knew things about God that no one else had ever known.

To most casual bystanders Jesus would seem no more than a poor Galilean carpenter who spoke well in the synagogue. But there was one at least who became aware that Jesus knew things hidden from ordinary human beings, and the implication was astonishing. "Rabbi," declared Nathaniel, "you are the Son of God!"[1] Earlier than this, John, the last prophet of Israel, affirmed, "I have seen and have borne witness that this is the Son of God."[2] Soon Martha would tell him directly, "I believe that you are the Christ, the Son of God, who is coming into the world."[3] Jesus himself said, "I am the Son of God."[4] And more mysteriously, "I came out from God."[5]

Does this mean that in some way God was divided or extended in order to remain in heaven and yet occupy a human body on earth? Perhaps it does, but our human language and earthly experience do not equip us well to understand what is possible for an infinite

---

[1] John 1:49
[2] John 1:34
[3] John 11:27
[4] John 10:36
[5] John 16:27

spiritual being. Jesus simply talked about his Father in heaven, and in doing so, told us more about God than we have learned from anyone else.

Above all, Jesus taught us that we are deeply loved. His Father is our Father too – not distant and indifferent but deeply interested in each of us. So we have this wonderful assurance: "The Father himself loves you."[1] He knows our failings and shortcomings. He hears all we say; he sees all we do, and loves us still. And loving us, he is concerned to provide for us. It is his pleasure to give good things to his beloved children: "Your Father knows what you need before you ask him."[2]

Jesus was undoubtedly a free thinker. He would make up his own mind about anything, and the conclusions he came to were highly unconventional. In fact his teaching turned everything upside down. Human kindness, he said, counts for more than religious ceremony. The simple faith of the poor is worth more than the lavish offerings of the rich. The things that people value highly are insignificant to our Father in heaven. Those who are last in the world become first in his estimation. The kingdom is not to be seized by people powerful enough to demand it, but given freely to those weak enough to long for it.

He taught that God condemns those who condemn, and forgives those who forgive. He hides the truth from those proud of their knowledge, and reveals it to those ashamed of their ignorance. And in the end, nothing, however unlikely it may seem to man, is impossible to him. All this and much more Jesus taught us about our Father in heaven, and how encouraging it is!

In a restless and unhappy world Jesus then gives each of us a most welcome invitation: "Come to me all you who labour and are heavy laden and I will give you rest. Accept my authority and learn from me, for I am gentle and lowly in heart, and you will find rest for your souls."[3] It is Jesus who shows us and then teaches us the love of God. We come to him, accept his authority, learn from him and so, at last, have rest.

What's Wrong with Me?

There was one thing that Jesus did not need to teach anyone. His generation, like ours, knew it well. The fact is that incompatible

---

[1] John 16:27
[2] Matthew 6:8
[3] Matthew 11:28-30

people cannot live happily together. Adam could not stay in the garden of Eden. Judas could not remain in the company of the disciples. There are certain behaviours which threaten and eventually end relationships. No one will choose to share a home with a person who is unpleasant or selfish or bad-tempered or deceitful. This may be a serious difficulty if we hope to draw near to God.

We do not like to think of it, but the people in our house know us as we really are. To avoid difficulties many prefer to live alone. Most of the time we suppress our bad attitudes and bad behaviour. But some people seem to bring out the worst in us. Some places bring out the worst in us. Some circumstances bring out the worst in us.

And where does that "worst" come from? Why is it so deeply rooted? Why does it rise to the surface? And how can I possibly be free of it? These are serious questions. If the Lord God is as good as we hope he is, how can I become compatible with him? How can I be the kind of person he would want to live with? Perhaps, after all, that "worst" is the real me, and I don't like it any more than he does.

This sense of alienation is our biggest frustration, and solving this problem was Jesus's first great achievement. Unlike those who bring out the worst in us, he brought out the very best in the people he was with. In his presence they were both attracted and appalled. For the first time in their lives they saw themselves as God sees them, and they did not like what they saw. Jesus did not need to say a word, but in his company they suddenly, desperately, wanted to be better men and women than they had ever been before.

With Jesus in his house, Zacchaeus became aware of the terrible contrast between himself and his guest. He did not need to be told he was greedy and corrupt. In his own heart he knew it and was overcome with shame. Urgently he resolved to put right all he had done wrong, to start a new and better life.[1]

Others were worse than Zacchaeus. So much harm had been done by them, they could not begin to put it right. With Jesus in his boat, Peter knew he could never be at ease in the company of one who knew his darkest secrets. "Go away from me Lord," he begged. "I am not at all a good man."[2]

---

[1] Luke 19:2-10
[2] Luke 5:8

But Jesus had other ideas for Peter, and for Zacchaeus – as he does for you and me. With him as their friend, each would have a chance to become a better person. Better indeed than they ever imagined they could be, for he would show them how.

A Fresh Start

In Jesus these men saw the living God. Attracted and appalled, they were astonished that he would still want them anywhere near him. But then for Zacchaeus, for Peter, and for many others, a day came when Jesus did far more for them than that. Already he had let them feel the shame, awakened an urgent desire for change and welcomed them as friends, but then he went much further. He carried in his own body the penalty for all they had done wrong. This much he told them himself.

Dying on a rough wooden cross, he paid the price for the gross and appalling wickedness of the world. He suffered the alienation that belongs to all mankind and so reconciled us to the eternal God. Few people understood it at the time although he explained it to them. "The Son of Man," he said, "came not to be served but to serve, and to give his life as a *ransom* for many."[1]

A ransom is a high price paid to liberate men and women from a desperate and dangerous captivity. In the chains of our human stupidity and selfishness, we were all held captive until that terrible and magnificent day when he ransomed us. Then "Christ suffered once for all the offensive things people have done. The innocent died for the guilty, so he might bring us to God."[2] That is what the Bible says.

All he ever asked in return is that we put our trust in him and devote our lives to him. That is all. Then he will bring us to God.

But how will he bring us to God? The answer could not be more simple. He looks for us and finds us where we are – incompatible, alienated – attracted and appalled. Then he simply offers himself to us, and for us. We may now come to the creator of the universe as friends and followers of Jesus and find acceptance for his sake.

So to each of us there comes the possibility of a fresh start, a new life. "He himself carried in his body on the tree all the offensive things that we have done, so we might die to such offensive behaviour and live to do what is right."[3]

---

[1] Mark 10:45
[2] 1 Peter 3:18
[3] 1 Peter 2:24

To accept this new life is to be born again, and it is a personal choice. It is between you and the Lord your God. You simply come as you are and ask him to wash away your own dark stain for the sake of Jesus who loved you and gave himself for you. Then you will have the joy of feeling clean in the sight of God. "If we confess the offensive things we have done, he is faithful and just to forgive our offences and to cleanse us from all we have done wrong."[1]

All this is clearly taught in the Bible. And when Jesus brings me to God, he does not introduce me to someone different or distant from himself. He simply welcomes me into the family circle where he rightly belongs as an integral part of the family. Indeed, if Jesus brings me to God, he brings me to himself, and in doing so makes me welcome anywhere and everywhere the infinite creator God is found. He brings me as close to God as any human can possibly be.

That is our first and greatest difficulty overcome, but there is another that may worry us even more.

An Astonishing Conclusion

It starts when we are quite young – surprised by unexpected illnesses, shocked by tragic accidents, distressed by so much pain. It gets worse in middle age, with pitiful loss of hearing, memory, mobility and sight. It moves inexorably towards dementia, breathlessness, heart failure and death. Can Jesus help us with the horror of our human disintegration and the universal terror of dying? Yes he can, for he has battled with death and overcome it.

For six long hours, as Jesus hung in agony on that wooden cross, his friends, his mother and other relations watched his life ebbing away until his final breath. Then having speared his heart to be certain of his death, the soldiers took him down. Laying his cold body in an empty tomb, the attendants rolled a heavy stone across the entrance, sealed it tight and set a guard.

Two days pass. Coming to the tomb in the early dawn, his friends are astonished to find it empty, the stone rolled away, the grave sheet still lying where it was. Then he himself is standing there, alive and well. A little later he comes to his disciples in the upper room, walks with two of them on the road to Emmaus, cooks breakfast for some others by the lake, teaches a large company on a hillside in Galilee. At first they thought it was a spirit or a ghost

---

[1] 1 John 1:9

but he reassured them, "See my hands and my feet, that it is I myself. Touch me, and see. For a spirit does not have flesh and bones as you see that I have."[1]

These friends of his were totally convinced that he had died and come back to life. But can we, so many years later, be sure of it?

The Roman army certainly knew how to execute a man, and they positively confirmed his death. The Jewish authorities admitted that his tomb was empty and his body gone; it worried and embarrassed them. That much is evident.

Then more than a hundred other men and women claimed they saw him alive in various places, his wounds healed, the scars still visible. They went out and proclaimed the news in the streets. When arrested they declared it in the law courts. Threats of imprisonment and martyrdom could not silence them. They insisted, "God raised him up, freeing him from the bitter pains of death, for he could not possibly be kept there in captivity."[2] Three thousand people in the city immediately accepted what they said, for the evidence was undeniable.

There must be many implications when a dead body comes to life but one consequence stands out above the rest. We can be absolutely certain of one thing. There is now conclusive proof that a human being can survive fatal injuries, loss of all vital functions, and death itself. A body may be broken, cold, utterly lifeless, and yet make a full recovery.

This happens so rarely that science has had no opportunity to observe the process of resurrection. We can only speculate concerning how a lifeless body might be repaired and reanimated. Is it feasible for each cell to be rebuilt from the genetic code stored in the mind of its creator, with every biological memory bank recovered and restored? And after that, is it possible for every organ to be activated and so come to life? If anyone can do this, the designer and maker surely can.

But what did Jesus himself say about all this? He declared, "An hour is coming when [not just one or a few but] *all who are in the tombs* will hear my voice and come out, those who have done good to the resurrection of life, and those who have done evil to the resurrection of judgment."[3]

---

[1] Luke 24:39
[2] Acts 2:24
[3] John 5:28-29

This is an uncompromising declaration that those great scourges of mankind – disease, damage, decay and death – can all be reversed and overruled. Just as he rose from the grave alive and well, so shall we. And what happens next for each of us depends not on the kind of people we are *then*... but the kind of people we are *now*.

This I Firmly Believe

The early Christians had many things yet to learn, but of some things they were absolutely sure. While continuing to discuss wider implications they held on to definite facts. There is much wisdom in this. However much we may doubt, there are always some things we can firmly believe. Such strong points will serve as anchors to stop us forever drifting.

If I need to build or to rebuild my faith I should begin by asking: What facts do I have? What can I be reasonably sure of? On a page in my notebook I will jot down a few things I believe to be highly probable or definitely true. These are matters I have thought about and settled in my own mind. Other more doubtful issues can be left aside for the time being.

Whatever I decide to write down is provisional, awaiting further confirmation. The following day some words may need to be crossed out, or others added. The next day there will be more changes. Certain things I will underline as I become increasingly sure of them. In this way my own statement of faith begins to take shape.

Each time I look through my notes, my confidence grows. I can affirm "That much is true" and "Yes, I believe this." Whatever I write and underline will provide a measure of stability while rebuilding other elements of belief. As more and more is settled in my own mind, my faith becomes increasingly secure.

Let's see how it goes. I might, for example, start by jotting down three things that make sense to me:

I believe the natural world was designed by an awesome intelligence.

I believe the Gospel writers have told us the truth about Jesus.

I believe Jesus has told us the truth about God.

These could be the first three points in my statement of faith. You may have written something quite different. So far so good. There will be more to add as we progress. But now we must look more closely at the meaning of faith itself.

Coming to Faith

"In every person's life there are moments when there is a lifting of the veil at the horizon of the known, opening a sight of the eternal. Each of us has at least once in his or her life experienced the momentous reality of God. Each of us has once caught a glimpse of the beauty, peace and power that flow through the souls of those who are devoted to him. But such experiences or inspirations are rare events. To some people they are like shooting stars, passing and unremembered. In others they kindle a light that is never quenched. The remembrance of that experience and the loyalty to the response of that moment are the forces that sustain our faith."[f]

Those are the words of a Jewish rabbi, a man seeking God in the way of his people. Faith, for him, is a personal response to a significant moment of insight or awareness. From then onwards, faith is sustained by the memory of that moment.

He is right. An awareness of God is like hearing a call. Faith then sends an answering call that changes everything. Awareness reveals an open door, but faith walks through that door and keeps on walking. Awareness may happen once in a lifetime, but faith will sustain and enrich all of life forever.

But there is something else equally important. We must understand that faith is more than mere belief. Belief may be no more than the passive acceptance of a probability or fact, but faith is a commitment. Indeed, it is a daring adventure.

I may *believe* in God and yet have no *faith* in him. I may be convinced he exists but have no real interest in him at all. I may *believe* the Bible is true but ignore what it says. I may even *believe* that Jesus died for me without it making any difference to me. Belief like this is static and inert; it takes me nowhere.

Faith, on the other hand, is a dynamic response of loyalty and trust – a commitment to a person who has won my confidence and respect. Faith is active, energetic and determined. To give one's faith is a promise. To break faith is a betrayal.

In the early stages of my spiritual journey, my faith may be in the mysterious intelligence whose creation astonishes me, or whose presence I have felt. Or it may be in Jesus whose character I admire and whose word I accept. But faith will grow to embrace all that I know of God, the God who made me and who became man to save me. My faith is faith in him. It means accepting whatever he offers, believing whatever he says, relying on his judgment, following his directions.

I cannot depend on someone else's faith or someone else's Saviour. I must be sure that when Jesus died, he suffered there for *me*, bearing what *I* have done wrong. And when he rose, he rose there for *me*, to assure me that *I* too will rise from death to life. As the thief cried out, "Jesus, remember *me*." As Mary said, "They have taken away *my* Lord." As Thomas declared, "*My* Lord and *my* God!" And Paul proclaimed "the Son of God, who loved *me* and gave himself for *me*." It is not enough to know that others have faith in him. I need him to be *my* Saviour and *my* Lord too.

Faith is a very personal thing. It is my commitment to him, to his ideals, his cause and his purpose for my life. It changes my priorities; each day asking, "Lord, what do you want *me* to do?"; each day offering, "Here I am! Send *me!*" This is my faith. It is my response to his call. It is my trust in him, my loyalty to him and my willingness to follow wherever he may lead.

My Fathers' God

My faith is between my Lord and me; no one else is involved at all. Yet when I put my faith in him I join the company of people in every age and place who have done the same.

Some of us have come to God as a consequence of evidences and insights, by means of a lonely quest and a profound conversion late in life. Others have come more gently, accepting as a child the faithful word of family, teachers or trusted friends. In one or other of these two ways we come with thankfulness to a knowledge of the truth.

Yet each of these alone secures no more than half a faith. What I have discovered for myself must be completed by what I learn from others. And what I have learned from others must be confirmed by what I discover for myself.

Moses once sang a song: "This is *my* God and I will praise him, *my father's God* and I will exalt him."[1] Moses did not imagine for a moment that he was the first or only person to make contact with the creator of the universe. The God he worshipped was his father's God; there was much he could learn from generations gone by.

---

[1] Exodus 15:2

You may come to faith on your own and then afterwards, to your great surprise, meet others who hold the same beliefs. Your God, you now realise, has been for many generations *your fathers' God*. Or your experience may be quite different. From childhood you heard Bible stories, simply and naturally believing every word, but years go by before you have your own encounter with the living God. You have always known he was your fathers' God but now he has become *your God too*.

A secure and settled faith will have these two bright facets. It is both a heritage and a quest, embracing what I learn from others and what I discover for myself. Starting with one, I must make sure to secure the other. Then he will be, for me, my fathers' God and my God too.

The Faith of Friends

If it happens that the living God reveals himself to me, that is no reason to start my own religion. To others he has revealed far greater things – things indeed that I cannot know, as they happened before my birth or in places where I have never been. There were eyewitnesses in the garden of Eden, on the slopes of Mount Sinai, in the stable at Bethlehem, on the Mount of Olives, at the place called Calvary and in the garden tomb. What these men and women tell me will become part of my own faith.

For Paul, "the mystery of our religion" meant things he had heard from others but never seen himself. Of first importance for him were the facts of Jesus's life: "He appeared in a body, was vindicated, was seen, was preached, was believed, was taken up in glory."[1] Those historic facts stood firm and immovable through all the changing circumstances of Paul's life. His temptations, persecutions, discouragements and triumphs could not alter the truth of what he believed and taught. The reliable testimony of others had become the strong point of Paul's faith. So it will of mine and yours.

In times of trouble this keeps us steady. When plans fall through, prayers go unanswered, friends let us down; when the suffering of loved ones seems pointless and unfair – with present circumstances confused and past insights forgotten – then may come the hard questions and the doubts. Where is God in this? Why would he

---

[1] See 1 Timothy 3:16.

allow it? Was I wrong to put my trust in him? And then in our darkest moments: What if there really is no God at all?

It is then that I most need reassurance and most appreciate the strength I find in the company of believers. As trouble rises up, or as tragedy bears down, I need not face it alone. With my own confidence shaken, I cling to the faith of friends I admire and family I trust. Others have been through times like this, held true to their beliefs, and indeed became stronger for the testing. They will have answers to my questions or comfort for my sorrows that I, for the moment, have forgotten, or never knew.

Yet no one can live forever on the faith of others. I must have a secure faith of my own. It is not sufficient to know that others are in touch with the living God; I need his help and guidance for myself. I cannot merely participate in my church's love for him or my family's love for him. I have a life to live with him myself. I must be sure that he loves *me*.

4.

Avoiding Error

In the history of the world, many religions have been born when a sensitive person became aware of a spiritual presence, invisible but real – a power in the air or in the heart, acting in nature or in man. Some have tried to capture and tame this sense of the sublime, to repeat the experience through rituals, and even to impose it on others through wars or laws or other forms of oppressive violence. And so the personal sense of wonder and mystery are lost and in their place grows up a religious and political system for controlling communities and nations. This is the universal tragedy of religion.

In some cases it was never a true encounter with the living God but with some other force, dark, devilish and deceptive. In other cases it may have been a genuine experience of the creator, afterwards perverted, exploited and abused.

In the quest for God it is possible for any of us to go astray. Security lies in taking our bearings from time to time and checking our position. This can be done in two ways: firstly by examining the sweetness of the fruit we bear, and secondly by comparing our beliefs with those of people we can trust.

First of all then, there is a simple question to ask: Is my faith making me a better person or a worse? Am I becoming more patient, more loving, more discerning, more sensitive to the needs of others, more like Jesus Christ? Am I becoming purer in heart and mind, wiser in word and deed? If so, there is good reason to suppose I am on the right track, that I really am in touch with the true and living God.

Then secondly, if we are walking in the truth, we will not walk alone but in company with all who know the truth, whatever their personality or culture or historical context may be. And naturally, if you claim to be a Christian, you are committed to believing what Jesus Christ himself believed and taught.

Basic to his belief was an acceptance of the Bible as a true record of what God has said and done and promised for the future. With the words "it is written" Jesus proved many things by authority of the prophets and the Law.[1] He affirmed, "Scripture cannot be broken."[2] To some who thought differently he gave this warning: "You are wrong, because you know neither the scriptures nor the power of God."[3] After his departure he expected his disciples' teaching to be equally reliable, for he told them plainly, "When the Spirit of truth comes, he will guide you into all the truth."[4]

So then, if my opinion contradicts Jesus himself or the consensus of Bible writers, there is good reason to suppose that I am wrong. And if they knew the truth, I will be wise to learn all I can from them. This requires careful research.

The Name of God

The word "God" is familiar to us, perhaps too familiar. It is an English word. When Abraham, Moses and the prophets became aware of a powerful divine presence, they did not call him God. They thought of him as *el*, or *elah*, or more frequently *elohim*, for they spoke Hebrew.

These are awesome words with a connotation of strength, grandeur and authority. They were fitting for the creator of all things, for one with power to provide and protect, and also at times to punish.

There is something especially mysterious about the word *elohim*. It is a plural, but always used with a singular verb and nobody knows why. It hints at complexities beyond our comprehension. An intense feeling of awe, uncertainty and perhaps fear would be inspired by the majestic, enigmatic *elohim*.

In the course of time Jewish communities were scattered through many Greek-speaking nations. Here the local people believed in hundreds of gods or *theoi*, many of them selfish, corrupt and

---

[1] Matthew 4:4; 21:13; 26:31 etc.
[2] John 10:35
[3] Matthew 22:29
[4] John 16:13

immoral. A single god would be a *theos*. Jewish settlers adopted this Greek word and began to speak of the *theos*, the true and living *theos*, the *theos* who made all things and then gave special promises to them. When the New Testament was written in Greek this was the word they used.

In western Europe people had many myths and legends about gods and goddesses. Germanic races spoke of Woden, Godan, Wod and God. The translator of the Gothic Bible in the fourth century adopted the local word *Guth* or *Guda* so that people would have some idea of what he was trying to say, and other early translators did the same. The words *theos* and *God* conveyed some idea of deity, but the awesome mystery, grandeur and authority of the Hebrew *elohim* were lost along the way.

In English Bibles and churches today the word *God* is used as though it were the name of our creator. But it is not his name; it was the name of a mythical deity, lifted out of legend and given to him. This was simply a translator's choice. But there is also a wonderful fact. He has a name. And we actually know his name, for he has told us what it is.

When we love or admire someone, the sound of their name brings pleasure and delight. If their name is mentioned across the room, we strain to hear more. If a street sign bears their name we point it out. Children have their hero's name printed on their shirt. Teenagers in love write their names on walls and trees. If we are seeking God, we will surely be interested in his name. If our desire is to love him, we will surely love his name.

The Bible writers expected this. David prayed, "Be gracious to me, as you are with all who *love your name*."[1] He begged for protection "so that those who *love your name* may rejoice in you."[2] And the creator himself offered special help: "I will protect him, because he *knows my name*."[3]

If that is so, it raises an obvious question: What is his name? Moses expected the Israelites to ask this very thing. In reply the Almighty declared, "I am who I am." And then, "Say this to the people of Israel, '*I am* has sent me to you.'" And making it even clearer, "Say this to the people of Israel, '*Yahweh*... has sent me to

---

[1] Psalm 119:132
[2] Psalm 5:11
[3] Psalm 91:14

you.' This is my name forever, and this is what all future generations are to call me."[1]

The name Yahweh, sometimes written as Jehovah, literally means "he is" or "he exists." But it could equally mean "he was" or "he will be". It is a word that embraces all of space and time – past, present and future – here, there and everywhere. It fixes no boundaries. Any other name would limit him in some way, requiring countless additional names to describe all his attributes, but *Yahweh* simply means he *is*. He exists. He simply *is*, always, everywhere.

In the same way that the mysterious term *elohim* evokes his awesome mystery and power, so the unfathomable *Yahweh* reveals him as unlimited and infinite, existing in realms of space and time far beyond the narrow constraints of our humanity. That is how all the Bible writers thought of him.

Proclaiming his Name

The Bible, of course, comprises two great collections of writings. First there is the account of primeval and Jewish history in the Old Testament, and then Christian history in the New Testament. In the Old Testament of the Jews the name *Yahweh* appears 6,823 times, and this raises a further question. Why in our own day do we not call our maker by his proper name? Surely by ignoring his name we lose an element of our faith and more easily forget what he is like. Why then, in our churches and schools, do we not call him Yahweh?

The reason goes back to early times and to the Law of Moses. Every Jewish community was taught, "You shall not misuse the name of Yahweh your God, for Yahweh will not hold anyone guiltless who misuses his name."[2]

The consequence of this was that instead of speaking his name with reverence and awe, most people felt safer not mentioning it at all. The rabbis never uttered the name Yahweh lest their hearers be tempted to repeat it lightly or flippantly and so incur guilt. He was always known to them as "the Lord". Whenever they took up the scroll to read and came to the word Yahweh, they said "the Lord". This Jewish custom is continued in our modern Bibles. Every time

---

[1] Exodus 3:14-15
[2] Exodus 20:7

you see "the LORD" in capital letters, you will be aware that the Hebrew text originally said "Yahweh".

With their Jewish heritage and their knowledge of Old Testament scripture, the early Christians would know the awesome wonder and burning purity of *elohim*, the infinite and eternal LORD. But later generations without this spiritual heritage might all too easily acquire a low and impoverished view of their creator. A *theos* or a *god* would not normally inspire much awe.

The same is true today. People around us seem to enjoy profaning whatever word they have for the one who gave them life and gives them every breath. Such is the strange perversity of human nature. To our generation the word *God* seems to have lost all meaning. It does not convey the breathtaking mystery, the penetrating clarity and creative power of the infinite Eternal. To communicate something of value to such people we must surely speak more clearly of "the Creator" or "the Almighty", or indeed "the Father" as Jesus did.

Yet among ourselves we have knowledge of his name. It is an astonishing privilege. When someone tells us their name we understand that they wish to be friendly or to say something important. If Yahweh tells us his name, we should take it as a wonderful gesture of friendship and a definite desire to tell us things we need to know.

Aware of this, we value and honour his name. We speak it with reverence and awe. Moses three thousand years ago declared, "I will proclaim the name of Yahweh."[1] Seven hundred years later Isaiah urged his people, "Give thanks to Yahweh... proclaim that his name is exalted."[2] And still today we can pray with David, "I give thanks to you, O Lord my God, with my whole heart, and *I will glorify your name forever.*"[3]

The Worship of Yahweh

An awareness of the presence of Yahweh may come to anyone at any time. I stand where I am in silence and in wonder. I gaze at the distant mountains or kneel on the forest floor and hold my breath with the beauty of the world around me. Every bird and leaf and every human being has been made with love and care. I think of my family and friends and happy times gone by and my heart is

---

[1] Deuteronomy 32:3
[2] Isaiah 12:4
[3] Psalm 86:12

filled with grateful thanks. Then come tears of relief and joy with the assurance that my maker loves me and cares for me. I see a plan for my life unfolding day by day and I am moved again with a sense of expectancy. Aware of the things I dislike about myself, I weep for my own stupidities. Then I recall how Jesus gave himself for me to wash away the past and bring me peace. In these moments I am overwhelmed by the wonder and the joy of the Lord. Is this what people mean by worship?

In the Bible we read of men and women who were moved to worship. The Hebrew verb *shaha* (*šaḥa*) means to bow down or kneel in reverence and in awe. So Abraham bowed to the ground and worshipped when three heavenly beings appeared to him at the oaks of Mamre.[1] His servant Eliezer bowed his head and worshipped as Yahweh answered his prayer and led him to the family he was looking for.[2] The Israelites in slavery, knowing their cry for help was heard, "bowed their heads and worshipped."[3] When Yahweh spoke from a cloud on the mountain, "Moses quickly bowed his head toward the earth and worshipped."[4] Joshua, suddenly aware of a divine presence before him, "fell on his face to the earth and worshipped."[5]

Such an experience would never be forgotten. All his days a man would live in the context of that moment. Without a doubt this is true worship. I suddenly realise I am in the presence of the eternal *elohim*; something astonishing has happened or is about to happen. I fall to my knees before him in amazement, gladly yielding to his purpose and his call. It is an unplanned and unexpected moment of encounter.

From early times people also brought offerings to the Lord God as a token of their thanks for his provision. Animal sacrifices were later prescribed by Moses to atone for various defilements. But then we come to a curious fact. The Law of Moses contains no command to worship. Although the Israelites in the wilderness were instructed to love Yahweh and serve him, they were never told to worship him. Only after they were settled in the promised land were they required to worship (kneel before him), and then just once a year as they presented the firstfruits of their harvest.[6]

---

[1] Genesis 18:2
[2] Genesis 24:26
[3] Exodus 4:31
[4] Exodus 34:8
[5] Joshua 5:14
[6] Deuteronomy 26:10; Leviticus 23:9-14

Time went by and the Israelites became familiar with ceremonies of worship performed by neighbouring tribes in magnificent temples devoted to idols and false gods. It was king David who first envisaged the construction of a temple for Yahweh supplied with ranks of musicians and priests to lead his own people in public worship.[1] But it was the later king Hezekiah who planned the most elaborate form of temple ritual. "He stationed the Levites in the house of Yahweh with cymbals, harps, and lyres... And when the burnt offering began, the song to Yahweh began also, and the trumpets, accompanied by the instruments of David king of Israel. The whole assembly worshipped, and the singers sang, and the trumpeters sounded. All this continued until the burnt offering was finished."[2] Proclamations were then sent throughout the land and the people of Israel summoned to attend temple worship in Jerusalem on designated days each year.[3]

This was a good thing in some ways, for the temple of Yahweh attracted people away from the temples devoted to idols and false gods. But at the same time it turned worship into a matter of ceremony and routine. Removed from the open spaces and mountaintops, confined to the inner chambers of a religious building, worship would now consist of elaborate rituals administered by priests, with disciplined performances from professional musicians and choirs. Worship had been tamed and domesticated as a public service at a designated time in a sacred place.

Yahweh himself expressed little pleasure in it, knowing indeed that such a system lends itself to complacency and hypocrisy, distracting his people from matters of far greater importance such as honesty, justice and the other aspects of good behaviour outlined in the Law.[4]

In Spirit and in Truth

Moving from the Old Testament to the New, we see the same process repeated. Worship, at first, was a spontaneous response of astonishment and willing submission to an extraordinary revelation of the Lord God. The Wise Men knelt in fascination and delight to

---

[1] 1 Chronicles chapters 22 to 29
[2] 2 Chronicles 29:25-28
[3] 2 Chronicles 30:1-27
[4] Isaiah 1:11-17; Hosea 6:6

worship the new born King.[1] A blind man, opening his eyes, saw Jesus and cried out, "'Lord, I believe,' and he worshipped him."[2] On a stormy sea, as Jesus came to them across the water, "those in the boat worshipped him, saying, 'Truly you are the Son of God.'"[3] After his horrible death and his burial he suddenly stood in their midst alive and well: "they came up and took hold of his feet and worshipped him."[4] Finally the host of heaven gaze appalled as a corrupt world is destroyed; then every one "fell down and worshipped God."[5] In each case, a sudden and overwhelming awareness of the living God brought a spontaneous response of amazement, awe and compelling faith.

With a spiritual heritage passed down from Abraham and Moses, these eastern semitic people all knew the meaning of worship, but later generations would not be so fortunate. Christianity was about to expand westward into a dominant Greek culture of competing myths, legends and philosophies.

The Greek verb used in the New Testament for worship is *proskuneō*. It originally meant something like "blowing a kiss", and this might be done to any statue or person. It is a far weaker word than the Hebrew *shaha* (to kneel or bow down in reverence and in awe). Again we see the shift from Hebrew to Greek weakening the sense of astonishment and wonder in the spontaneous worship of the Infinite and Eternal.

But what of the Jewish temple ceremonies still functioning at that time? When a woman remarked that Samaritans worshipped in one temple and Jews in another, Jesus did not encourage worship in either place. He replied, "The hour is coming, and is now here, when the true worshippers will worship the Father *in spirit and truth*, for the Father is seeking such people to worship him."[6] When his disciples admired the great stones of the temple compound, Jesus warned that the massive pillars and decorative arches would all be thrown to the ground.[7] Whenever he entered the temple area himself, his purpose was not to worship but to teach.[8]

---

[1] Matthew 2:11
[2] John 9:38
[3] Matthew 14:33
[4] Matthew 28:9
[5] Revelation 19:4
[6] John 4:23
[7] Matthew 24:1-2
[8] Matthew 26:55

The earliest Christians saw things in the same way. If they went to the temple, it was not to attend the priestly services but to gather in the outer courtyard among the teachers and money changers where they could discuss the good news about Jesus with passers-by. One of them was bold enough to remind the Jews that "the Most High does not dwell in houses made by hands."[1] He was stoned to death for saying it, but it remains the truth. His chief persecutor later admitted, "The God who made the world and everything in it, being Lord of heaven and earth, does not live in temples made by man."[2]

Those early believers did not make worship a duty. In fact they did not meet for worship at all but simply visited one another in their homes for teaching, fellowship, breaking of bread and prayer.[3] Here there was freedom for each to contribute a hymn or a prayer or an exhortation for the encouragement of all, not as a ministry to God but to one another.[4]

Time passed and those days were forgotten as the churches of Roman and Medieval times developed into powerful political institutions. These great religious establishments, Catholic and Orthodox, took their lead not from the early Christians but from the later Israelites, not from the New Testament but the Old – with priests, robes, sanctuary, altar, sacrifices and choirs in magnificent religious buildings. Just as the worship of Israel had become an elaborate public ceremony, so now was the worship of Christendom. Christian worship had become a service, and so it remains in many places today.

From the Depth of my Heart

We have seen how Jesus taught us to worship the Father, not in this temple or in that but in spirit and in truth, wherever we may be. In the forest or the garden I become conscious that he is there. I no longer search for reasons to believe; his presence is all the proof I need. Humbled and expectant, I ask him to guide my thoughts. There is no barrier between us. I tell him my troubles and my concerns. I confess my failures and my fears. I remember once again how Jesus died to bear my guilt and shame. I am accepted,

---

[1] Acts 7:48
[2] Acts 17:24
[3] Acts 2:42
[4] 1 Corinthians 14:26

loved and set apart for a special purpose. I am profoundly thankful. From the depth of my heart I worship him in spirit and in truth.

Later I become aware of him involved in the activity of the day. Observing a strange coincidence, I realise he has intervened. In a moment of sudden danger, I find he has kept me safe. Untangling a knotty problem, I see he is answering prayer. After a shameful mistake, I am given another chance. Opening the Bible, I find a verse that speaks to me. Far from home, I meet a fellow-believer who becomes a friend. In these moments I see my Lord at work in my life and again I am moved to worship in spirit and in truth.

Now at last my restlessness has gone for I have come to rest in him. The discovery that my heavenly Father loves me has changed my life. From then on I seek him in the quiet places, in the quiet moments of the day, or in the quiet company of his people, to read and think and be wonderfully refreshed.

I find true worship flowing from my heart, moving me to pray or sing in words inspired by his own Spirit in me. When he is with me, forgiving me, guiding me, helping me, loving me, I cannot merely repeat someone else's words, or pray someone else's prayer, or sing someone else's song. I must speak to him myself, in spirit and in truth. It is the truth that moves my spirit and inspires me. I hide nothing from him. I mean every word I say.

Aware of his presence and his love, I feel profoundly thankful for so many things. My instinct at such a moment is to find something I might offer. It may be a candle, or a prayer, or a bunch of flowers, or some money, but all these are inadequate and do not satisfy the need to give. Part of me or my possessions will not do; it must be more than that. So I humbly offer myself to the One I have discovered, the One who has discovered me. I give *myself* – to do anything, to go anywhere, to play my part in his mission for the world.

I still cannot really know him as he is – the creator of all things, the mysterious *elohim* who always is everywhere – yet in his presence I am perfectly content. His call is not for me to *know* him but to *love* him. Indeed, the Bible says, "If anyone imagines that he knows something, he does not yet know as he ought to know. But if anyone *loves* God, he is *known by* God."[1]

If I can simply get as far as loving him, that will be enough. If I love him... and he knows me... then a relationship of trust is possible between us.

---

[1] 1 Corinthians 8:2-3

TO LOVE HIM

5.

What is Love?

Love for our heavenly Father may come easily to anyone who feels loved by him. For some however, the idea of loving the creator of the universe raises more difficulties. These we must consider as honestly as we can.

According to Jesus the most important of the commandments is this: "You shall love the Lord your God with all your heart, with all your soul, with all your mind and with all your strength."[1] But what exactly does that mean? And is it really possible? How can I love someone I have never seen or heard? How can I love someone who is infinite and everywhere? How can I love someone who is already busy with seven billion other people?

Then other issues may come to trouble us. How can I love a God who allows so much suffering in the world? How can I love one who stands by when the innocent are hurt and the weak oppressed? How can we love a God who is not answering our prayers for peace on earth or even peace in our own family? These are important questions. But our first concern is to work out what we mean by "love".

---

[1] Mark 12:30

There is much talk of love in our world and much striving to love God in our churches. But what does love mean? Is it a feeling? Is it a duty? Is it something that comes and goes? Can we control it? Can we increase it? Is it something that only happens to emotional people?

Love is a word used to describe many different things. Parental love warms the heart as we pick up a new-born baby or play with a cheerful toddler. Romantic love stirs our hormones when we meet an attractive person of the opposite sex. Compassionate love moves us to carry a bag for an old lady or to help someone who has fallen in the street. We even say we love a particular piece of music or type of chocolate or item of clothing. We think we know what love is.

Yet love for God does not fit into any of these familiar categories. Yahweh is an invisible spirit, and if I am honest I cannot easily imagine how to love an invisible spirit. I can love my wife. I can love my children. I can love my friends. I can even love my enemies. But to love an invisible spirit seems quite beyond me unless I have some special help.

Then again, love may not always be what it seems. Every day on our TV screens people in strange clothes sing about love, describing passionate thrills and heartbreaks when they do not mean a word of it – and gaining both fame and wealth in the process. In every film there is at least one steamy scene of physical passion. Love has become a public performance, a commercial product, a form of entertainment – and for many people love is little more than that.

In church too we may sometimes sing about love. But for most of us this is not natural. It is not normal human behaviour. True love between a man and a woman, or between friends, or between a mother and her baby, is not normally sung into a microphone and amplified. It is not printed in a book or projected on a wall. Genuine heart-felt love is spoken quietly, sincerely and very privately. There may be profound emotion, but it is not for public display. If we ever tell others about it we will speak of it shyly and hesitantly, because real love is a very private thing. We do not boast about it.

The meaning of love is further complicated by our modern culture and its grotesque obsession with sex. Love for Jesus expressed by female singers and worship leaders can sometimes seem romantic or frankly erotic. Intrusive homosexual agendas in politics and the media can bring an awkwardness when a man speaks of his love for the man Christ Jesus. Childhood memories of an angry or uncaring father may make it hard for some to express any positive feeling for a heavenly Father.

All this tends towards confusion and anxiety in our efforts to love the Lord our God. We are left with questions. Can a man have a healthy manly love for Jesus his Teacher and Friend? Can a woman have a healthy womanly love for her spiritual elder Brother? Can we all have a healthy childlike love for our heavenly Father? And if so, how can we deepen and express this love and make it a genuine part of our personal faith?

All this we will consider, but first there are some more urgent and basic hindrances to clear away.

A Great Hindrance to Love

It will be much easier for me to love the Lord my God if I can be absolutely certain that he loves me. We each need assurance of this, and not one of us can take his love for granted. The issue of alienation and compatibility arises once again. If I have caused offence to him in any way, love becomes much more difficult. Before we can live happily together I must be assured that all is well between us. If not, a relationship of trust will remain elusive and unfulfilled.

Tension between me and my heavenly Father may go back to a disappointment, a resentment, a moral lapse, an unhealthy obsession, or simply a routine of Christian duty that has stifled the wonder and the joy. I may have made a bad choice that cast a shadow on my life, or mixed with people who led me seriously astray. Or I may have started grumbling and complaining, and making myself thoroughly disagreeable to him. If so, there is some preliminary work to be done before I can even think of loving the Lord my God or enjoying his love for me.

In his youth David was known to be a man after God's own heart. He prayed and sang to Yahweh while guarding the flocks of sheep. But after he became king, David lay with another man's wife. Then he murdered her husband. At first he pretended he had done no harm, but the words of a faithful friend helped David to see himself for what he was. Then he felt ashamed and unclean, wretched and contemptible in the sight of his maker. He had done something terribly wrong and now could do nothing to put it right. "Have mercy on me, O Elohim," he cried, "according to your steadfast love... Create in me a clean heart, O Elohim, and renew a right spirit within me. Do not banish me from your presence! Do not take your Holy Spirit from me!" Bitterly aware of his weakness and his need: "Restore to me the joy of your salvation," he begged, "and strengthen me with a willing spirit."[1]

Many others have faced a crisis of this sort. If you have wronged someone or caused offence to the eternal God, deal with it quickly before the wound festers and poisons your spiritual life for ever. Give back what you have taken, mend what you have broken, apologise for what you have said, put right what you have done wrong, as far as you possibly can. Turn to the Lord your God. Kneel before him and confess. Weep if you must. Plead with him to forgive and cleanse and restore you. Then remember that Jesus was nailed to the cross in your place so you could walk free.

Here then is the first and greatest hindrance to love – my own selfish stupidity. But then the astonishing experience of being forgiven and welcomed back may awaken, for the very first time, a love for my Lord that remains with me all my life.

Set Free to Love

For others the hindrance to love may be far less dramatic. Perhaps you have simply become caught up with issues that complicated your life, deadened your spiritual awareness and led you away from the Lord your God. They may have been good and worthy causes – social concerns, the environment, political or economic programmes, or particular doctrines of importance in the church. Or it might have been something more selfish – the passion for success, wealth, power or excitement.

Anything that takes over your life will become a tyrant, driving and controlling you as a master drives a slave. It can destroy your marriage, your family, and your friendships; it can ruin your health and bring you to an early grave.

Jesus said, "No one can serve two masters... You cannot serve God and money."[2] But other more noble causes may just as easily narrow your spiritual horizon, change your personality, and deaden your ability to love. Jesus once sent a message to a church more interested in hating what was wrong than loving what was right. Unless they changed their priorities, he warned them, their church would have its light put out. Before long it was indeed left in

---

[1] Psalm 51:1, 10-12
[2] Matthew 6:24

darkness.[1] If you have become a person driven by an agenda that has enslaved or embittered you, it is time to rethink your agenda before it is too late.

But that may not be your case at all. You may have been trying for many years, with humility and genuine compassion, to serve the Lord your God. You are simply worn down by routines of Christian service, weary with the duties and obligations of a busy programme in church or mission – a committed member but no longer a healthy or a happy one. You might sympathise with one overworked pastor who suffered a breakdown and then admitted, "I was a bit surprised to discover that God had been, in many ways, a stranger to me. Maybe that's why it's so hard for some of us to trust God in a crisis: we are forced to commit ourselves to Someone we don't know very well."[g] Those are the words of a well-meaning but very weary man.

To feel any love for God in your present condition may seem a forlorn hope. The problem, however, is neither with you nor with him but with the circumstances that entangle you. It is time perhaps to reassess your commitments and discover what is truly important. Or simply take a holiday in a quiet place and let your heart and mind regain their equilibrium. That is not even wisdom but merely common sense.

Communicating Love

To *believe* in the invisible God is easier for most people than to love him. We are familiar with the idea of believing in things we cannot see. We believe in electricity and in gravity. We believe in proteins and vitamins, atoms and molecules simply because others have told us about them. But we do not normally *love* the things we believe in. And they do not expect us to love them, because naturally none of them claims to be a person. But the invisible Spirit whom we call Yahweh is different. We are supposed to believe in him and also to love him.

In normal family relationships and friendships, love can be expressed in various ways. We will show love for one another with positive words of affirmation, with time spent doing things together, with thoughtful and appropriate gifts, by helping in practical tasks, and by warm and affectionate physical contact. But applying these ways of expressing love to our relationship with the

---

[1] Revelation 2:4-5

eternal *elohim* becomes difficult, if not impossible – and for one simple reason. Love between parents, children, husbands, wives, friends and strangers is communicated first of all with the eyes and the tone of voice and of course with a friendly smile. We pick up the subtle signals that people are warmly disposed and interested in us. We read the body-language; we sense the love they have for us, and this makes it easy to respond with love. Everything else is secondary. Words, time, gifts, help, touch will all be meaningless if there is no twinkle in the eye and no tenderness in the voice.

On these terms, when we seek God's love we have a problem, for we cannot see his welcoming smile or hear his cheerful greeting. There is no handshake or hug. With Yahweh we lack the basic means of sensing and receiving love that we depend on every day of our lives in our relations with other people. There is no body-language; there are no signals to pick up.

This distressing lack of signals may trigger a desperate search for some kind of response from heaven simply as proof that God loves us. It sometimes brings a craving for emotional ecstasies, prophetic affirmations, miraculous gifts or physical manifestations. Manipulation and delusion may easily follow. But if this danger is foreseen and avoided, how can we genuinely experience his love for us, and how can we express love for him? If we cannot see him, hear him or touch him, how can we really love him?

The Most Loving Person

The answer is found in Jesus. In the streets of Jerusalem and the fields of Galilee people picked up the human signals. They could see the welcome in his smile, hear the gentleness of his voice, observe the play of emotion in his eyes, feel the positive warmth of his hand and the compassionate strength of his arm. They could read his sensitive body language. They knew exactly what he felt and where they stood with him.

We can be certain of this because they have told us about it. John recalled how much "Jesus loved Martha and her sister and Lazarus."[1] Peter observed his reaction to the words of an earnest young man: "Jesus, looking at him, loved him."[2] Others noticed the tears he wept for a friend who had died: "See how he loved him!"[3] Every day Jesus showed his affection for them all. "As the Father

---

[1] John 11:5
[2] Mark 10:21
[3] John 11:36

56

has loved me, so I have loved you," he said. "Live always in my love."[1] The same quality of affection would be seen in those who followed him. "By this," he said, "all people will know you are my disciples, if you have love for one another."[2] Then finally they watched him lay down his life for them all: "Having loved his own who were in the world, he loved them to the end."[3]

Before Jesus came among them, the disciples had the same problem that we have with the invisibility of God. "No one has ever seen God," they admitted, but then, to their great relief, "the only Son, born from the heart of the Father, he has made him known."[4] One of them begged him, "Show us the Father, and we shall be satisfied." To which Jesus replied, "Whoever has seen me has seen the Father."[5] In the very visible Jesus they could see "the image of the invisible God".[6] They could see what God is like.

Now if anyone had dared suggest to those men and women that God was cruel or unloving or impassive or aloof, they would utterly deny such a strange idea. In Jesus they had seen his true nature, and Jesus was by far the most loving and caring person they had ever met. At times he spoke very boldly; at times he felt very deeply. He was grieved, he wept, he rejoiced. With a strong and positive touch he laid his hands on the sick and blessed the little children. He showed them the love of God, not as a mystical dream but as a way of life, a strong, bold, positive love in action.

And how did the disciples respond to this love? One said, "I will follow you wherever you go."[7] One declared, "I will lay down my life for you."[8] Another urged, "Let us go too, that we may die with him."[9] Love flowed constantly between Jesus and his friends. They could see the honest face of love; they could hear the sincere voice of love, and their response was evident in the intensity of their loyalty to him. Having seen and heard, they could never doubt his love for them. And loving him, their greatest desire was to be worthy of his love.

---

[1] John 15:9
[2] John 13:35
[3] John 13:1
[4] John 1:18
[5] John 14:8-9
[6] Colossians 1:15
[7] Matthew 8:19
[8] John 13:37
[9] John 11:16

But how does all this help us today? To start with, it shows how easily and naturally love kindles love. That was true then as it is now. The disciples, like us, found it much easier to love the warm-hearted human Jesus than the invisible spiritual Yahweh. Understanding this, Jesus simply told them, "Anyone who loves me will be loved by my Father."[1]

You Have Not Seen Him

How greatly privileged were those disciples, the friends of Jesus! And how deeply we may regret we do not live in that land and in those days! If only we could see and hear Jesus himself, we would surely love him, and learn to love his heavenly Father as he did. But we live in a different time and place with our own troubles and concerns, and we do not have him here to help us.

This became a problem almost immediately for the early Christians. Peter wrote to a new generation in a distant land who had heard about Jesus and accepted what they heard. He carefully reassured them, "Though you have not seen him, you love him. Though you do not now see him, you believe in him and rejoice with a joy too great and glorious for words."[2]

A little later he encouraged them again, addressing a second letter "to those who have received *the same precious faith* that we have ourselves."[3] Unlike Peter they had not lived with Jesus for three years, yet Peter saw no difference between his faith and theirs. They did not need to see Jesus in order to love him. They did not need to hear his voice in order to believe in him and rejoice with a joy that ran too deep for words.

Our own experience shows how we can love someone without seeing them or even knowing where they are. A husband or wife travelling far from home will be loved just as dearly as if they were here in our own living room. Absence is even said to make the heart grow fonder. A lack of physical contact or visual presence need not diminish love or weaken our fondness, loyalty and affection.

And yet, you may say, we have at some time seen and heard and embraced our family and closest friends. Even Jesus was once seen and heard by the people around him and they felt his touch. We can imagine what it was like for them to love Jesus. But for us he is

---

[1] John 14:21
[2] 1 Peter 1:8
[3] 2 Peter 1:1

just a character in a book. We have never seen his smile or heard his voice or felt his warm embrace.

This might seem a great handicap to love. And yet there are characters in books we have never met but who have engaged our interest and sympathy, our admiration and affection. We love them dearly although we have never seen their face or heard their voice. At times we cannot bear to put the book down, we are so concerned to find out if they are still safe and well. And if they should chance to die, we may mourn their death for days. Yet they may be entirely fictional with no real existence at all.

This shows us something very curious about ourselves. We are able to love someone we cannot see or hear. We can love someone we have never seen or heard. We can even love someone who is imaginary. If that is so, there is no reason why we should not feel a genuine attachment and warmth towards the real living person whose name is Yahweh revealed to mankind in Jesus Christ.

And he is certainly not just a character in a book. He is present with us now wherever we may be. If your faith is in him, then his Spirit is in you. "Do you not know that you are God's temple and that God's Spirit dwells in you?"[1] He becomes your closest friend and you may feel his presence every waking moment of the day. We will speak more of this.

---

[1] 1 Corinthians 3:16

6.

A Measure of Love

As human beings our feelings change from day to day and hour to hour. We are cheerful when health is good but discouraged when things go wrong, pleased when the postman brings a parcel but annoyed with an unexpected bill. We feel much better on holiday than we do at work, better in a restaurant than a traffic jam, better after taking a shower than before. Our morale is even influenced by the weather and the seasons of the year. But how does this affect our love for God?

Many will freely admit to frustration with the emotional ups and downs of their spiritual experience. There is a great warmth of devotion one day and a strange indifference the next. We love God well enough in church but can't seem to find him anywhere at home or work. We love him enthusiastically at a conference or a camp but do not feel the same when teaching Sunday School week after week. Others long to recover the feelings of first love that they enjoyed many years ago but lost somewhere along the way. For all of these, the meaning of love may be unclear.

We naturally feel more positive when things go well. The fact is that we are often more loving when things go badly. It is a child's illness that brings out the tenderest care in her mother and father. It is when the pipes burst that a neighbour becomes a really good neighbour. It is when the old lady falls that her children rally round to care for her. For most of us, we hardly know what love is until things go wrong.

To think of love as a feeling is a mistake that many people make. When we are most loving we may not feel much love at all. As

Jesus was nailed to the cross, it was pain he probably felt far more than warm affection, and yet it was love for us that led him there. Such love is not pleasant. Love gives until it hurts for the sake of the beloved.

In middle age some of us, fearful of losing our first love, try hard to revive the passion of our youth. To be excitable and passionate is quite normal for the young, but few of us were really more loving in our teens and twenties. With the passing years we naturally calm down, and if our energy is rather less, our knowledge and discernment may be far more. A kind old gentleman of eighty may do more real good than a fiery zealot of eighteen. We should expect to lose our first passion without losing our first love.

There is no doubt that some people think of love for God as an exciting experience to enjoy. By means of fasting or acts of humiliation, or by shouting and chanting, they have hoped to be caught up to the third heaven, to see wonders, to fly with angels or to battle against demons. But this is not what the Bible writers mean by love. Love for God is not a private indulgence or a heavenly vocation. It is not a personal ecstasy or a mystical adoration. It is not reserved for a privileged few; it is a way of life for all. We are all, without exception, called to love him and to know his love for us as we go about the affairs of daily life.

It should be obvious that love is not measured by loudness or body temperature or energy expended or calories consumed but by the practical help, the comfort and happiness we bring to others. Love seeks nothing for itself but all for the beloved. That is how we should expect to love our heavenly Father, and how we might expect him to love us. Passion and pleasure may come and go with the passing hour, but love embraces all of life. Love is as consistent as the air we breathe. At times we simply need to breathe more deeply in order to do what must be done.

To Love and Be Loved

Once that is clear, some more complex issues may come to light – personal things that make it difficult to love the Lord our God or to experience his love.

To start with, it may be hard for me to love him simply because I am not a loving person. I have never learned to love with genuine unselfish love. I have never been concerned for the happiness and well-being of anyone except myself.

Naturally this means I am incompatible with a God of love. "Anyone who does not love does not know God, for God is love."[1] Pitiful indeed is a man or woman habitually cold and cynical, or critical and angry, and incapable of real kindness or affection. It is very obvious: "He who does not love his brother whom he has seen cannot love God whom he has not seen."[2]

If conflict has become my way of life, I cannot help being in conflict with him too. If my mind is focused on my own rights and privileges – harsh and unpleasant with neighbours and shopkeepers –cursing other drivers on the road – unforgiving towards my family – how dark and clouded will be my perception of a loving God.

And yet, whatever we may be like, God himself is love. That is the character he has. When other people behave badly, he loves with patient, understanding, steadfast love. Such love is strong enough to overwhelm the dark unlove of man and win over people who are critical, unkind and unforgiving.

Among the early Christians was one who bitterly condemned himself for the bigoted cruelty of his past life. Paul could never forget how he had hated the followers of Jesus, broken into their homes, imprisoned and beaten and passed sentence of death on them. He had been harsh and angry, prejudiced and callous. Then suddenly he encountered the risen Lord. To his astonishment Jesus spoke kindly to him, accepted him as he was and then changed him for ever. "But I received mercy for this reason," said Paul, "that in me, as the very worst, Jesus Christ might display his perfect patience as an example for those who would later believe in him for eternal life."[3]

If this obnoxious man could be truly forgiven, there is hope for every one of us. If Jesus will help me, I really can become a new person with a new personality. That is what Paul himself discovered. "If anyone is in Christ, he is a new creation," he said. "The old has passed away; see, the new has come. All this is from God, who through Christ reconciled us to himself."[4] That is what his love can do for me and you.

With a new life and a new personality, a whole new way of living opens up. You begin to greet people cheerfully; you thank them warmly; you overlook their minor faults; you lend a hand

---

[1] 1 John 4:8
[2] 1 John 4:20
[3] 1 Timothy 1:16
[4] 2 Corinthians 5:17-18

wherever you can. Then comes the marvellous discovery that the more you love others, the more they love you. For indeed, as Jesus said, "The measure you give will be the measure you get."[1]

In your own experience, love has kindled love. And the more you love people, the happier you are – and the easier it is to love the Lord your God. That is certainly a wonderful surprise.

Learning to Love

Some people have a completely different problem. They are not cold and unloving. On the contrary, they are enthusiastic lovers, but their love is misdirected. There is no place for the Lord God in their life simply because their love is spent and exhausted on other things.

One great concern of the Bible writers was the issue of idolatry, and this may seem quite irrelevant in our modern age. Yet the significance of idolatry lay not in its quaint carvings of wood and stone but its massive investment of loyalty and devotion in the wrong place. The people offering sacrifices in the idol temples were intelligent, creative and extremely energetic, but their efforts were focused on objects that achieved nothing of lasting value. It was a costly investment with poor returns. They were riding, as it were, at high speed, an exercise bike which took them nowhere.

The majority of us already love, and love perhaps to excess. We love a football team, or a fine wine, or holidays in the sun, or a view from a window, or a piece of music, or a new car, or even our work. There is a sense of delight, a desire to look again or to listen a second time, a longing to tell someone about it. We know what love feels like, but our love is misplaced. It exhausts its precious energy on the challenge of the workplace or the pleasures and pastimes of our leisure hours. Our problem now, as in ages past, is simply idolatry. Our love is lavished and wasted on the wrong things.

It is curious that not one of us is born with an interest and a love for any of these delightful occupations and activities. Each of them is an acquired taste. The more attention I give to a sport or a musical instrument or a piece of work, the more I become engrossed in it.

The acquiring of these personal tastes and preferences is often a deliberate choice. A prisoner, to pass the time, will take up wood

---

[1] Matthew 7:2

carving. A girl will interest herself in her boyfriend's sport. A child may be persuaded to start piano lessons. A husband will try to appreciate his wife's artwork. Many things in life we learn to love. By asking the names of garden flowers, we become more inclined to do some gardening. Reading newspaper reports of a local team, we think about going to a home match. Identifying some garden birds, we begin to value and enjoy wildlife. The more we know about these things, the more interesting they become and the more we find we love them.

Many people have never given much thought to the creator and sustainer of the universe simply because they are busy with other things. They have never taken the trouble to enquire and find out, and so have no idea how interesting life becomes when he is at the heart of it. If some of the extravagant energy we devote to our personal idols were offered instead to the Lord our God, what great things we might accomplish in this world, not merely for our own pleasure but for the benefit of mankind! With a growing interest in him, all sorts of possibilities open up. We will speak more of this.

A Matter of Fact

In our own experience we know many different kinds of love and draw a distinction between them all. We have thought of parental love and compassionate love, and also the more mundane love of activities we enjoy. We love the friendship and good company of a youth group or a social club. Then someone special comes along and we fall in love.

Our love for the Lord our God is different again, and cannot be identified with any of these other familiar loves. Its closest parallel is probably found in families. My mother loves me because I am her son, and I love her because she is my mother. We belong to each other. I did not choose her and she did not choose me. Our relationship began because one day I was born to her. Its basis is a fact that neither of us can change. As the years went by she cared for me as a good mother would and I cared for her as a good son should, so we each gained many more reasons to love and honour and appreciate one another. These too are facts in the history we have shared together. In consequence of all this, her love for me, and mine for her, has become steady, loyal and committed.

Very similar to this is my love for my heavenly Father. It exists because of what has happened between us. Its basis is a fact, followed by many shared experiences. He thought of me and made me, loved me before I was aware of it, suffered greatly for me, accepted me when I was weak and helpless, and now lovingly provides for me. I feel secure in his love, happy to recall everything he has done for me, and eager to please him in return.

I could not claim to be worthy of such love. Painfully aware of wasted years and times I have let him down, I could never say, "I am good enough. I deserve to be loved by God." Yet he has set his love on me. "See how much the Father has loved us, that we should be called God's children – *and so in fact we are.*"[1] If I am accepted as a child of the living God, that will be – for me – an astonishing privilege.

This is the essential point. It does not depend on what I do for him, but on what he has done for me. I could spend all my life attempting to do good and religious things in order to be acceptable to God, and still never be sure I had done enough. Doubt, anxiety and frustration would be the sure result. But when Jesus paid the price for me, he cried, "It is finished!" And so it was and always will be. He is my Saviour and with him I am safe. I have been born again and adopted into his family.

A Declaration and a Promise

It seems right and fitting that a new relationship of such permanent importance – like a birth or a marriage – should be sealed with a declaration and a promise. When Jesus died to atone for the guilt and shame of this chaotic world, he forged a new covenant between God and man. A covenant is a binding commitment, and when I put my faith in him I enter into that covenant.

This is the greatest privilege ever offered to a human being. It is not given to everyone. Indeed, many are unaware of it, and some refuse it. As a turning point in my life, it will be natural to mark it in some way and share it with the people who are closest to me.

In his final instructions to his followers Jesus asked them to baptise every new believer in water. Baptism would symbolise two things which he had done for them.

Firstly, he had washed them cleaner than they could ever wash themselves from the guilt and shame of all they had done wrong. "He saved us," they confessed, "not because of good or religious things we have done, but by his own mercy, through the washing

---

[1] 1 John 3:1

of rebirth and renewal through the Holy Spirit."[1] This Holy Spirit is the Spirit of Yahweh, the Spirit of Jesus, who comes to renew us from within. As soon as we put our trust in him he starts that work of renewal.

And secondly, he had raised them from a condition of death to spiritual life forever. "We were buried with Christ in baptism," they declared, "and so shared in his death. Then just as he was raised from death by the glory of the Father, we too will live a completely new life."[2]

When I am sure of this for myself, I will be glad to make it known. I may ask to be baptised in a lake or river, or in a house or church building. Baptism does not make me a member of anything; it does not change me in any way. It is simply my personal declaration of commitment and belief.

There is no obligation to invite friends, neighbours or relations to watch, but if they are willing to come they will more easily understand what has happened to me. They may have questions. They may take a liking to my Christian friends. They may even decide to throw in their lot with us. Then they may ask us: What is it really like, to be loved by the eternal God?

---

[1] Titus 3:5
[2] Romans 6:4

7.

Our Father's Love

There is more love in the Bible than we hear from many preachers and writers. A sermon may often mention the love of God in passing but rarely is a talk devoted entirely to this most encouraging and essential subject. Books of systematic theology will present arguments for the existence and character of the Almighty but the table of contents and index will include few, if any, references to love.

This may be why we think so little of our heavenly Father's love for us. We are not convinced of his interest in his beloved children. We have not been taught about his personal affection for us. And yet, throughout the Bible, love is what motivates all his dealings with mankind. Without appreciating this, we may fail to grasp what is happening in the Bible at all. It is time to open the book of books and look more closely at what it says about the love of the eternal *elohim* for the people he has placed on planet earth.

Although many tribes and nations have had female deities, the God of the Bible is always uncompromisingly "he". Jesus confirmed this by speaking consistently of "my Father" and of course by teaching us to pray "Our Father…" In what ways then is he like a father?

A good father is one who provides for his children, protects them, teaches them, disciplines them, and guides them through the stages of life. He opens doors, pulls strings, cheers them on and catches them when they fall. A boy or girl with a strong and supportive father has many advantages in life and is likely to grow up balanced, sensible and successful.

Some of us as children did not have such a positive experience of fatherhood. This is sad and cause for regret, and yet to the people concerned it has often proved less disastrous than we might suppose. An unhappy childhood has caused many to think more carefully about parenting and indeed to picture what an ideal father would be like. Many a man has become an excellent parent by carefully avoiding the mistakes suffered in his own childhood. And if I have never known the love of an earthly father at all, the love of my heavenly Father may come as an even more wonderful and unexpected surprise.

When Jesus and his early followers thought of Yahweh as a father, they envisaged the highest ideal of fatherhood and the best of all possible fathers. They would expect him to provide for his children's needs, to protect them, teach them, discipline them and guide them through the stages of life. Like any good parent, he would open doors, pull strings, cheer them on and catch them when they fall. To feel warm respect and love for such a father would be the most natural thing in the world.

The early Christians did not find it hard to love their heavenly Father and they often spoke of his love for them. If he was the King then they were the children and heirs of the royal household. They saw themselves as "the children of the kingdom", set apart "to inherit the kingdom he promised those who love him."[1]

This meant very special privileges – for indeed, "no mind has conceived what God has prepared for those who love him."[2] Every morning such children would anticipate his generous provision, his wise advice and his careful protection. And every evening they would thank him for his gifts, his guidance and his safe-keeping.

The early Christians had seen their Father bring good out of every experience they went through. They could happily affirm, "We know that God works all things together for good to those who love him and are called according to his purpose."[3] These men and women had heard the call of Yahweh and given him their love. They saw a purpose in their lives and could trust him to fulfil it. That is the kind of father we all need, and to our great comfort and delight the Father that we have.

---

[1] Matthew 13:38; James 2:5
[2] 1 Corinthians 2:9
[3] Romans 8:28

Words of Love

As we have seen, the word "love" carries many diverse meanings and is sometimes much misused. In English, however, we cannot easily find a better word that people will understand. Every teacher and translator faces difficulties of this sort, because the words available to us often seem quite inadequate to convey what we really want to say.

The same was true in Bible times. When the Bible writers spoke of love they were obliged to take existing words and add as much value to them as possible. The Israelites were fortunate in this regard, having several good words in Hebrew to express various aspects of love, enabling them to understand a great deal about it. We will look at five of them.[h]

In the Old Testament the commonest word for love is the noun *'ahaḇāh*. It speaks of an emotional attachment and desire, a commitment of loyalty offered whether or not the loved one is worthy of it or even wants it. This word describes Yahweh's intense love for the people he had chosen, and also their love for him. So he says to them, "I have devotedly loved you with a devoted love that is everlasting. So I have continued my faithfulness to you."[1] How wonderful it would be for anyone to know they are loved with such *devoted* love!

Another word for love in the Old Testament is the noun *ḥeseḏ*, expressing steadfast loving kindness. It is the love of an established relationship, based on a covenant or promise. There is a sense of obligation sought and willingly accepted. So a prophet might say to Yahweh, "You will show faithfulness to Jacob and steadfast love to Abraham, as you have sworn to our fathers from days of old."[2] How privileged we would be to have this relationship of *steadfast* love!

Then we come to the noun *raḥamīm*, meaning compassionate love, a spontaneous feeling of pity or affection. It is a love that forgives. So we read, "Yahweh is good to all and his compassionate love is over all that he has made."[3] How greatly we need the warmth of this *compassionate* love!

The verb *ḥāshaq* (*ḥāšaq*) is much rarer, meaning to set one's love on someone or to desire someone. It is a deliberate love and

---

[1] Jeremiah 31:3
[2] Micah 7:20
[3] Psalm 145:9

appears in a significant passage where Yahweh says to the Israelites, "It was not because you were more in number than any other people that Yahweh set his love upon you and chose you, for you were the fewest of all peoples; but it is because Yahweh loves you and is keeping the oath which he swore to your fathers."[1] How marvellous would be the security of such a *deliberate* love!

Then finally the verb *ḥānan* describes gracious love, dealing favourably with someone whether or not they deserve it. So we read, "The Lord is merciful and gracious, slow to anger and abounding in steadfast love."[2] How much we need to be forgiven and accepted with this *gracious* love!

From their own experience the writers of the Old Testament had learned a great deal about the eternal God. With these five Hebrew words they described his love as devoted, steadfast, compassionate, deliberate and gracious. They saw how actively he seeks to form relationships and covenants with those he loves in order to secure a mutual commitment of loyalty and faithfulness. In response to his all-embracing love for his people, he asks them to love him in the same way – with loyal, consistent, steadfast love.

Many of them did. So for example we hear David, rescued from his enemies, declaring, "I love you, O Yahweh, my strength. Yahweh is my rock and my fortress and my deliverer."[3] An unknown writer would echo this, saying "I love Yahweh, for he has heard my voice and my cry for mercy."[4]

Other people, however, were much less open to the love of the eternal God. Some needed to be warned, "Be very careful, therefore, to love Yahweh your God."[5] It is significant and sad that in the Old Testament much more is said about Yahweh's love for his people than their love for him.

Loyal Steadfast Love

Turning then to the New Testament we come upon a curious fact. Although a number of well-known Greek words for love already existed in the works of playwrights and philosophers, the writers of the New Testament rarely used any of them. In the pagan literature of those days the commonest Greek words for love are *storgē*

---

[1] Deuteronomy 7:7-8
[2] Psalm 103:8
[3] Psalm 18:1-2
[4] Psalm 116:1
[5] Joshua 23:11

(family fondness), *philiō* (friendly attachment), and *erōs* (passionate desire) but none of these words expressed what the early Christians understood of God's love for them or their love for him.

They opted instead for a word that had become widely known through the Greek translation of the Old Testament (the Septuagint). This is the noun *agapē* with its associated verb *agapaō*. Among the Greeks it was not a strong word and did not express great vigour or depth of feeling. But in Jewish communities speaking Greek the word *agapē* had gained an emotional intensity from its use in Bible passages of great power and beauty describing the love of God. All the energy of the Hebrew *'ahaḇāh* was packed into the Greek *agapē*.

Intense devotion and loyalty are essential to *agapē* love. It expresses Yahweh's love for his own people and their love for him. It is love freely given – a generous and purposeful love and indeed a commitment to the welfare of someone whether or not they show themselves worthy or responsive. This is what *agapē* love meant for Jesus when he said, "No one has greater love than this, that he lay down his life for his friends."[1] A few weeks later that was the love he gave them.

As for the other four Hebrew words, their nearest equivalent in Greek was usually the noun *eleos*. In secular literature this meant mercy or kindness, but when the Old Testament was rewritten in Greek, all the strength and vigour of the Hebrew prophets would again be loaded into this word. To its first readers it expressed the awesome wonder of the steadfast, compassionate, deliberate, gracious love of the eternal *elohim*.

So we see that the Israelites and the early Christians did not speak of their relationship with Yahweh in terms of fondness or friendliness or passion. That is not what the Bible means by love for him. We love the living God when we are committed to him and set our hearts to seek him and to please him. We love him when we are loyal and faithful to him. That is what the Bible means when it asks us to love the Lord our God. And that is what it means when it speaks of his love for us.

---

[1] John 15:13

Who Loved Me

In many of the stories Jesus told, he portrays the love of God, and in some of them this love is quite emotional. Love indeed is an emotional thing. To lose what we love is very painful. To find it again brings great joy.

So Jesus described the feelings of a shepherd whose lamb is found, a woman whose coin is recovered, a father whose wayward son returns. And then he says there is joy like this in heaven whenever a lost soul is found and brought to safety. Vividly and unforgettably he shows us the depth of his Father's love for human beings in their most wayward and degraded condition. It is a tender personal concern that goes in search of us when we are hopelessly bewildered and off-course, and a great warmth of affection that delights to have us safely home. When Jesus tells these stories he is speaking from experience. He has felt that joy; he knows that love.

Our Father is still in search of men and women who will worship him in spirit and in truth. He comes gently, kindly, offering help if we want it, ready to withdraw if we do not. He reveals something of himself and waits for a response.

That is how he comes looking for you. In the stillness of evening there comes a peace that calms your troubled heart. Or a tiny mouse sits beside you without fear and you see that all creation has been designed and made with love. Or you hear the Bible carefully explained and recognize the truth of what it says. Or you fall in love and realize that romance is a gift from one who loves and knows everything about love. He comes to you when you fail and most urgently need comfort and fresh hope. He comes to you when you are happy and for the first time in your life offer him your thanks.

Suddenly you become aware that you are deeply loved. The love which had already convinced your mind has now won your heart, altering not just the way you think but the way you are. As one of the Bible writers said, "We have come to know and to *believe* the love God has for us."[1] You knew it before in theory but now you believe it with all your soul.

For some of us, this awareness remains longed-for and elusive. We believe what we know but still seem to feel very little. This may be a problem from the past. Perhaps all feeling has been numbed by failure, sorrow or distress. The only way forward is to

---

[1] 1 John 4:16

take his love on trust. Whether you feel it or not, you are deeply loved by God.

He loved you when he created you with your own personality and unique potential. He loved you before your birth, kept you safe through all those years, and taught you everything you need to know. He has brought you to this present moment and now comes to help you with the next stages of your life.

He loved you before you had any thought of loving him. He was concerned for you while you were a grief and an offence to him. "God shows his love for us in this: While we were still offending against him, Christ died for us."[1] It could not be said more clearly: "While we were enemies we were reconciled to God by the death of his Son."[2] He planned and prepared and suffered for you while you were ignoring or even opposing his purpose for your life.

Even now his gift of love is offered to the least lovely, to the most unlovable, to those who have never perhaps felt loved by anyone. Such a woman, with years of sleazy living behind her, was found by Jesus and wept with relief and joy to know she was loved by the God she had so long offended.[3] Saul of Tarsus, with his many cruelties forgiven, never forgot his encounter with "the Son of God *who loved me* and gave himself for me."[4]

To discover that God loves me as I am (with all my failures and regrets), and to find that he has plans for me, will change my life for ever. It led that happy woman to honour Jesus publicly at risk of insult and ridicule; it carried Saul throughout the world proclaiming the truth he had discovered to any who would listen. It might do the same for you and me.

Children who Are Loved

In the Bible, God is simply described as "love". Indeed this is almost a definition. "God is love."[5] He is not just loving, or inclined to love; he is himself love personified. There is no word in our English language that better describes him. Whenever we think of the eternal God, our first thought of him is love.

He loves us whether we are lovable or not. He loves us because it is his nature to love. We do not have to persuade him to be

---

[1] Romans 5:8
[2] Romans 5:10
[3] Luke 7:36-50
[4] Galatians 2:20
[5] 1 John 4:8

sympathetic or compassionate or kind, because that is always how he is. The reason we know anything about love is simply because he has made us in his image and therefore capable of love. "We love because he first loved us."[1]

We have seen how love takes pleasure in giving the very best to the beloved. A loving husband will think how to please his wife. A loving wife will think how to please her husband. Each will offer the best they have to one another, and to their children and their friends and neighbours. In the same way, our heavenly Father is glad to offer his very best to us.

This does not mean we always understand what he is doing or appreciate his gifts. He knows what his children need and provides exactly that. Jesus said, "If you who are far from perfect know how to give good gifts to your children, how much more will your Father in heaven give good things to those who ask him!"[2]

In the course of daily life, a good father will explain the options and alternatives to his children and help them discern for themselves the difference between sense and stupidity. He will teach them how to make sound choices, exercise self-discipline, invest time and effort wisely, judge when a risk is worth taking, avoid serious errors and injuries, deal fairly and sensibly with other people and so to succeed in life. In the same way, through experiences, both pleasant and unpleasant, our heavenly Father will teach us to be perceptive, poised, focused and consistent.

We are encouraged to pray at any time for any thing we need. "Ask," said Jesus, "and it will be given to you."[3] But our Father will not grant our most selfish wants and whims. A spoilt child is one who has been allowed to manipulate his parents and so becomes selfish, vain and deceitful. No one can manipulate the eternal *elohim*. He will do everything to help us grow up well, to become complete and mature in character, to achieve our full potential as men and women of God.

We might expect an intelligent child to take notice of a good example and sound advice, but not all are so intelligent. And many lack the determination to resist peer pressure and powerful temptation. At times, in order to secure the safety of a daughter or a son, a father may need to warn and explain – and then perhaps to forbid. If all else fails he will enforce discipline, reducing

---

[1] 1 John 4:19
[2] Matthew 7:11
[3] Matthew 7:7

privileges and increasing pains until the lesson is learned the hard way that might have been learned more easily.

This is how our Father deals with us. He will help and also hinder so we develop our strengths and overcome our weaknesses. Through what happens to us he will build into our character the qualities we need, preparing us to achieve our full potential and become the people we can be. He makes sure we grow strong and wise, gentle and persevering, compassionate, considerate and self-disciplined. He brings out the best in us and expects the best of us. All this he does for his children because he loves each one of us as only a perfect Father can.

But there is one more thing, and this is among his greatest gifts. As soon as you have Yahweh for your Father you become a member of his family. Now you have brothers and sisters, young and old, far and near, who are glad to see you and enjoy your company.

Each of them is special, accepted and loved by him and by one another. They will welcome and support and care for you, helping you in many ways and teaching you many things. They will encourage you to make progress, widening your horizons with opportunities to be useful in their company and in the world around.

This may come as a surprise and a great delight. Knowing I am accepted and valued and honoured among such special people, I have a deep longing to be worthy of their love, and to love them as deeply as they love me.

If Anyone

In all his teaching Jesus made faith a very personal matter. He taught us to think about individual choices, attitudes, habits and beliefs. This was one of his great innovations.

When crowds came to hear him he focused on "each of you". He singled out "every one who asks". He identified "the one who hears the word" and "anyone who is not offended". He asked, "Which of you, having a son...?" or "Which of you desiring to build a tower...?" And many of his parables addressed issues of individual responsibility and opportunity.

In modern English the word "you" will serve either for one person or for many. This can be very confusing. It means we easily miss the point when Jesus addresses a crowd and emphasizes "you yourself", asking each man or woman to make a decision or response. His meaning is much clearer in the old Authorised Bible of 1611 with its archaic "thee" and "thou". "When thou prayest..." "If thy right hand offend thee" "If thy brother hath aught against thee..." "If thine eye be evil..." Jesus intended all this to be intensely personal.

The importance of this is often overlooked. It is not enough to belong to a covenant nation or a priestly family or a good church. It is through personal faith that I have peace with God. I stand or fall in my own right on that account. In "the book of life" are written the names of believers, not of nations or families or churches. Jesus said, "If anyone has ears to hear..." "If anyone would come after me..." "If anyone keeps my word..." The offer is for you yourself, to be accepted or refused.

Just as it is a personal thing to believe in Jesus, so it is a personal thing to live each day with the Lord your God. There will be private dealings between you and him that no one else knows about. If you pray it will be in secret "and your Father who sees in secret will reward you." If you help someone it will be in secret "and your Father who sees in secret will reward you." If you fast, you fast in secret "and your Father who sees in secret will reward you."[1] This is the teaching of Jesus.

Then if I have done wrong, I will speak directly to my Lord: "God be merciful to me the offender." If I am in trouble I will cry, "Lord, please help me." If I am grateful I will say "I thank you, Father, Lord of heaven and earth."[2] Nothing could be more personal than that.

The Abundant Life

When I put my trust in Jesus I start to live with God. His Spirit begins to inspire some radical changes in my personality, my attitudes, my convictions, priorities and loyalties. "The Spirit himself bears witness with our spirit that we are children of God."[3] That is as it should be. Indeed, "Whoever does not have the Spirit of Christ does not belong to him at all."[4]

Now that my life is in his hands, I find to my amazement he is interested in all I do. In every decision I ask him to guide me. In every difficulty I ask him to help me, and he does. I find myself

---

[1] Matthew 6:1-6, 17-18
[2] Luke 18:13; Matthew 15:25 and 11:25
[3] Romans 8:16
[4] Romans 8:9

thinking differently about my circumstances and the people I am with. I see possibilities in myself and in the world around me. I become aware of better ways to act and to react. I realize what can be accomplished by gentleness, patience and compassion. I begin to see the power of right and wrong to build or to destroy. I learn the value of purity, honesty and truth. I discover how much good a little generosity can do. I become aware of better options, wiser choices and fresh directions. I am seeing the world and everything in it with fresh eyes.

My longing is now to become a better person, more like Jesus, more like my heavenly Father, more like my friends and family who truly follow him. That's what we would expect for all who belong to Jesus. "We all, with unveiled faces, reflecting the glory of the Lord, are being transformed into his likeness from one degree of glory to another. For this comes from the Lord who is the Spirit."[1] It is not our doing but his doing in us.

Then I begin to see the people around me not as they were, or as they are, but as they might be if only they were loved a little more. And this is entirely natural, for "God's love has been poured into our hearts through the Holy Spirit who has been given to us."[2] His love is changing not just the way I think but the way I am. My personality is intensified, enriched and rounded out with his own strength of character given to me. Previously I was undoubtedly lacking something; now I have become "complete in him".[3]

And yet I am still recognisably myself. My personality is still my own, and no one could mistake me for someone else. I may be an active person like Martha or sensitive like Mary. I may be bold as Peter or thoughtful as John. I may be blunt and direct like Thomas, diffident like Philip or more outgoing like Andrew. Each of the disciples was born and raised with the exact personality God gave them, but each was then profoundly influenced by close contact with Jesus. And each, after his departure, would be refined, intensified and inspired by his Spirit to become what he intended them each to be. They were the same people as before but empowered with new life.

Many astonishing discoveries will follow in the course of this life but nothing matters so much as possessing the life itself. Jesus called it abundant life, and so it is. Now that I am living with the

---

[1] 2 Corinthians 3:18
[2] Romans 5:5
[3] Colossians 2:10

Lord my God, I can raise my head among people who reckon they are better than me. In the eyes of the world I may be a nobody, yet my heavenly Father loves me, guides me, strengthens and purifies me, and every day provides for me. I have become a very special person, very special indeed to him and to his people.

This is how I learn to live with God. Just as he has always known me, I am learning to know him. Just as he is aware of my concerns, so I become aware of his concerns. Now I am in touch with the eternal *elohim*, not as a theory or as a fact but as a person. And with a person I may have a relationship. Everything I see and hear and do, I see and hear and do *with him*. Every experience is shared. He knows what is happening, and he is involved.

8.

Is Anyone in Control?

In these days newspapers, television and cheap novels bombard us with subtle allusions and crass assumptions that God is irrelevant and that those who believe are either corrupt or stupid. It takes some considerable effort to swim against the tide and say, "Wait a minute. Do you know what you are talking about? Does your lack of respect merely show your prejudice and your ignorance? And what do you gain by undermining the faith of thousands who find great comfort in their beliefs?"

All the same, year after year, these attacks can wear us down. God may love the world but what difference does he really make? We know from experience that a kind and loving person may be powerless to help or to protect. In some circumstances love is not enough, if it has no power to intervene and take control. Is this all we can really expect of God – a little sympathy or regret?

In the heat of the battle between good and evil, there is much noise and confusion, and the majority may seem to be against us. We cannot tell if the course of events will swing this way or that, or who in the end will win. The onlooker might conclude that God himself is powerless to intervene. He may be loving, but is he in reality so weak and insignificant that we would be unwise to look to him for help and foolish to depend on him for anything?

The Bible writers have an uncompromising answer to this question. In fact they have more to say about the power and authority of Yahweh than about his love. Having created the universe, he sustains it; he directs it, redistributes the people upon it, and at times he condemns and removes tribes, nations and individuals. To Jeremiah he says, "It is I who by my great power and my outstretched arm have made the earth, with the men and animals that are on the earth, and *I give it to anyone I choose*."[1] Jesus, when challenged by the Roman governor said "You would have no power over me unless it had been *given you from above*."[2] The Almighty is indeed all-mighty. Job said, "I know that you can do all things, and that no purpose of yours can be thwarted."[3] Jesus agreed. "All things are possible with God," he said.[4]

But the power of Yahweh to intervene and take control is not random or capricious; it is purposeful and exercised for the benefit of his people. Many times we read, "they cried to Yahweh in their trouble, and he delivered them from their distress."[5] When Jerusalem was threatened he declared, "I will defend this city to save it, for my own sake and for the sake of my servant David."[6] So Mary the mother of Jesus sang her song: "He has scattered the proud in the thoughts of their hearts; he has brought down the mighty from their thrones and exalted those of humble degree; he has filled the hungry with good things, and the rich he has sent empty away."[7]

This world may seem out of control but the Bible writers have reason to think the opposite. "I know the plans I have for you, declares Yahweh, plans for welfare and not for evil, to give you a future and a hope."[8] The eternal *elohim* not only knows the future; he secures it. "I am God," he says, "and there is none like me, declaring the end from the beginning and from ancient times things not yet done, saying, 'My counsel shall stand, and I will accomplish all my purpose,' calling a bird of prey from the east, the man of my counsel from a far country. I have spoken, and I will bring it to pass; I have purposed, and I will do it."[9]

But this raises a further question. If Yahweh is truly in control, why does he not keep us safe from harm and danger in the world he has so carefully made?

---

[1] Jeremiah 27:5
[2] John 19:11
[3] Job 42:2
[4] Matthew 19:26
[5] Psalm 107:28
[6] 2 Kings 19:34
[7] Luke 1:51-53
[8] Jeremiah 29:11
[9] Isaiah 46:9-11

Weeds among the Wheat

In these present days, as indeed throughout human history, it is evident that vandals, terrorists, profiteers and fools are at loose in this unhappy world. Many good ideas and great plans are carelessly spoiled or deliberately wrecked. Jesus told a story in which a farmer sowed good seed in his field. At night someone came and sowed weeds among the wheat. The servants came and said to him, "Master, did you not sow good seed in your field? How then does it have weeds?" He replied, "An enemy has done this."[1]

From early days the Bible writers were aware not only of Yahweh working for good in his creation but also an unseen enemy working actively for evil. This is "the adversary" (satan, or *satanas* in Aramaic), also known as "the accuser" (devil, or *diabolos* in Greek).

It is clear that we may sow good seed and pray for a good harvest but then, on account of an enemy, see our hopes frustrated and our field spoiled. And this problem, Jesus warns us, will not be resolved before Judgment Day.

We suffer with our Lord the profound sorrow of seeing his creation in constant danger and disarray. Many good intentions and noble projects are undermined or crushed. Jesus himself, teaching his disciples, was troubled by one who became a traitor. Paul, as he preached good news, suffered "a thorn in the flesh... an agent sent by satan".[2] Others were warned, "The devil is about to throw some of you into prison."[3] Most of us are handicapped in some way. It is what we achieve against the odds that makes our lives heroic.

But why would the eternal *elohim* withdraw his protection from what he has so carefully made? Why would he allow an enemy to wreck it? We imagine there must be some compelling reason, and indeed there is. The troubles we face make us aware of something we really need to know. They serve to remind us, and to ensure we never forget, that we are held accountable for what we do. When our earliest ancestors chose to disobey God, the whole world was changed. The earth became a dangerous place for mankind. They wanted a knowledge of both good and evil, and that is what they

---

[1] Matthew 13:27-28
[2] 2 Corinthians 12:7
[3] Revelation 2:10

got. They began to suffer disease, damage, decay and ultimately death.

As human beings we are survivors of one judgment and preparing to face another. That will be the last judgment, the final judgment when the whole world is called to account. After that, there will be no further judgments, no more danger, decay, disaster or death, for the earth and everything in it will be made new. At present we live in a disordered world, preparing for a world restored to order, and preparing ourselves to live in it.

And yet, despite the chaos, the Master has not abandoned the field, nor the good seed growing in it. He has workers watching night and day to limit the harm that can be done. If our enemy is unseen, so too are the angels of the Almighty, thousands and thousands of them, according to the Bible, "spirits who serve God and are sent by him to help those who are to receive salvation."[1]

As we pray each day for safety, corrupt people and occult powers are held in check, unable to reach the children of God. "The Son of God keeps them safe and the Evil One cannot touch them."[2]

And yet as long as this world lasts there will be injustice and people who suffer through no fault of their own. In every conflict there are bystanders caught in crossfire and peacemakers whose efforts are despised. It is at the final harvest that all wrongs will be put right. "Let both grow together until the harvest," says the Master, "and at harvest time I will tell the reapers, 'Gather the weeds first and bind them in bundles to be burned, but gather the wheat into my barn.'"[3]

Not till that great harvest day will all the accounts be paid and justice done. Not till the wheat is safely gathered in will its true value be assessed. And so we read, "If you are doing good and suffering for it, that is something very special in the sight of God."[4] It is something he will not forget.

A New World Coming

No doubt we are kept safe from many dangers – many indeed that we are not even aware of. And yet the suffering of the world around us continues without ceasing, an endless cycle of corruption, tyranny and war.

---

[1] Hebrews 1:14
[2] 1 John 5:18
[3] Matthew 13:30
[4] 1 Peter 2:20

We have already wondered why our creator does not step in to solve the problems of planet earth. Why doesn't he simply put an end to disease, decay and death? There is a reason.

We have a global problem which requires a global solution. In many places people are seeking not to limit corruption, tyranny and war but to exploit these for their own advantage. In fact things could be much worse. As things stand, every conqueror and oppressor eventually suffers illness or gets old and dies. But in a world with no disease, decay or death, a tyrant would continue in robust health to exploit and enslave his people and neighbouring peoples for ever and ever. If there were just one bully with this permanent immunity, he would take risks unthinkable to ordinary mortals; he would outlive all his rivals and become ruler of the world.

This makes one thing clear. The earth can only be healed when every last germ and parasite is gone. We will only be safe when every trace of evil is removed from our planet and when all its inhabitants are totally transformed. Our world cannot be put right until *everyone in it* wants it put right. Only then will it stay right.

This, of course, has never yet happened, and many people assume it never will. But Jesus, possessing inside knowledge, has told us it will be done, and done indeed by fire. Our fragile planet will be burnt to ashes, and paradise restored on the surface of the globe. "I came to cast fire on the earth," he said, "and how I wish it were already kindled!"[1] His close friend Peter knew what he meant. "The heavens and earth that now exist are being reserved for fire," he said, "being kept until the day of judgment and destruction of the ungodly."

Those final minutes are described in detail. "The heavens will pass away with a roar, and the elements will be burned up and dissolved, and the earth and everything on it will be laid bare." Then just as Yahweh made the old heavens and earth long ago, he will create for us a new world: "new heavens and a new earth inhabited by all that pleases God."[2]

On the new earth there will be no selfish, exploiting, violent, oppressive people, for all have perished in the fire. Human nature itself will be changed. Not one of earth's survivors will ever wish to exploit or oppress or harm another.

---

[1] Luke 12:49
[2] 2 Peter 3:7,10 and 13; see also Revelation 18:8; 21:8

Those who are chosen to repopulate the planet and re-establish its technologies, economies, sciences and arts will be raised from death with bodies that never grow old, ready to live as Jesus taught us to live, in his kingdom. "He will wipe away every tear from their eyes, and death shall be no more; neither shall there be mourning, nor crying, nor pain any more, for the former things have passed away."[1]

The facts are as clear as this. The inventor will reprogram his creation so it never breaks down again. We might say the world will be reformatted, the software upgraded and reinstalled. It may sound like science fiction, an imaginative utopian dream. Yet science fiction has often foreseen what later came to pass. And when the Bible writers predicted all this, they knew nothing of science fiction. They simply wrote what their Lord had shown them, believing it will happen exactly as he said.

And of course, if a creator made this world, there is no reason at all why he should not mend it, and every reason for us to listen carefully when he tells us how.

Better is the End

That is how the Bible writers saw it, but can we add anything that will make sense to our own generation? If Yahweh is perfectly loving and supremely powerful why are we left to face so many difficulties and bear so many bitter sorrows, seemingly on our own?

Truth is said to be stranger than fiction, but fiction may sometimes illuminate truth. Imagine a storybook where the prince and princess meet, get married, have plenty of children and live happily ever after. Is that book likely to become a best-seller? Or imagine a biography in which the main character has a normal childhood, finds a reasonable job, gets married to a nice girl, has a couple of children and eventually retires to enjoy a relaxed old age. How many of us would be content with a life so comfortable that there were no obstacles to overcome, no knots to unravel, no exploits to accomplish, no victories to win? The idle rich in past times went mad with boredom, or suicidal with the tedious monotony of a comfortable life; in these days they turn more often to drink or drugs.

---

[1] Revelation 21:4; see also 1 Corinthians 15:35-57

Every skilled author leads his characters through dangers and difficulties. That is what makes the story interesting. A handsome prince must climb walls, leap chasms, fight dragons, outwit ogres, find a golden key and open a dungeon door before he can rescue the beautiful princess. There is something in human nature that is only satisfied when solving problems and overcoming difficulties. That is why we spend hours with crossword puzzles, detective mysteries, jigsaws, quiz shows and card games; that is why we are devotees of the fishing rod, the racing bicycle and the golf course. Some go so far as white water rafting, bungee jumping or climbing mountains with crampons and ropes. We like a physical challenge which is also a test of character.

So far so good. We enjoy overcoming obstacles; but we also like a happy ending. It is the anticipation of the "happily ever after" that makes the pain and the trouble and expense worthwhile. The eternal God is writing a story. It begins with the book of Genesis, and it ends with the book of Revelation. Our chapter is somewhere in the middle. When things look black, we might do well to sneak a look at the final page, just to reassure ourselves that *all God's stories have a happy ending.*

The life that he gives you does not promise to be easy. You will have problems to resolve, opportunities to seize, frustrations to overcome. There will be challenges that bring out the best in you, or the worst. How you deal with them is up to you. But there is no fear that we will be tested beyond our strength. From experience, one of the Bible writers affirmed, "God is faithful, and he will not let you be tempted beyond your ability, but with the temptation he will also provide the way of escape."[1]

That does not mean we will always know exactly what is going on, or why. On one occasion Jesus himself said, "What I am doing you do not understand now, but afterwards you will understand."[2] There are reasons hidden from us that will one day be made clear. Limited we undoubtedly are in our knowledge and perception, but the God who made all this was there at the beginning and he will be there at the finish. "I am the Alpha and the Omega," he says, "the first and the last, the beginning and the end."[3]

As every inventor will know more than his invention, we would expect him to understand many things at present hidden from

---

[1] 1 Corinthians 10:13

[2] John 13:7

[3] Revelation 22:13

mankind. We should learn a measure of humility when discussing these questions. We can guess perhaps, or speculate, about why he has allowed his creation to become a constant challenge and a threat to us. Was it so that we might grow in strength of character through the challenges we face? Or that we might bear one another's burdens and so discover the meaning of love? Or that we might despair of ourselves and cry out for help to him? Or so we might look forward with keener anticipation to the day when this old world gives way to one far better, and prepare ourselves and others for that day?

As Solomon the wise observed, "Better is the end of a thing than its beginning, and the patient in spirit is better than the proud."[1] The happy ending is all the happier for the challenges which have been faced and the obstacles that have been overcome. But we cannot know the whole story until we turn the final page.

---

[1] Ecclesiastes 7:8

9.

A Growing Relationship

A relationship is a living thing which grows. With care and nourishment it will prosper. With neglect and indifference it will die. The more we open up to another person, the more they will open up to us. The more we share and enjoy together, the stronger will be our affection and attachment to one another

Experience shows that making relationships is not a science but an art. A scientist through logic may formulate a theory, and through measurement establish a fact, but when that scientist wishes to make friends with real people he does not use scientific methods. Friendship does not deal in logic or measurement but in sympathy, generosity, kind enquiry and warm response, with just an occasional hint or suggestion or request.

It was not logic or measurement, nor was it knowledge or even insight that changed the lives of the first disciples; it was their decision to follow Jesus. Living with him, life took on a different meaning. Fresh possibilities opened up; old habits faded away; new priorities and plans took shape. Jesus had won their confidence. Their desire was now to believe what he believed, to understand what he taught, to live as he lived in the love of his heavenly Father.

Every relationship, to start with, is tentative and provisional. With very few people do we immediately become the best of friends. It takes time to explore the character, the temperament and interests of another person. Trust itself must grow.

Although our first overtures of human friendship are usually cheerful and optimistic, we protect ourselves with inner reservations, always prepared to pull out if necessary. Two people will shake hands and talk of pleasant things, looking for what they might have in common, avoiding issues of tension and controversy. As we get to know one another, we weigh up whether or not to develop the friendship, to offer an invitation, to keep in touch. Minor peculiarities and irritations will be overlooked if the person seems reasonably congenial and interesting. After meeting a few times and enjoying one another's company, mutual confidence grows and becomes well established and finally unshakable. By then we say, "I know him well... he will never let me down... I have the utmost faith in him... We are the best of friends."

Through these same stages we may progress at first in our relationship with the living God. To start with, it may seem we are taking stock of one another, looking for what we may have in common, trying to decide if we will get on well together. As I discover what he is like and what he is doing in the world, my interest in him rapidly grows. I feel I would like to be added to the circle of his closest friends.

It may seem presumptuous to speak of friendship with the eternal creator of the universe, and yet he chose to call Abraham his friend.[1] He spoke to Moses as a man speaks to his friend.[2] Even Job recalled how "the friendship of God was upon my tent."[3] And Jesus assured his disciples he accepted them not as servants but as friends, hiding nothing and sharing everything with them.[4] Jesus liked these men, enjoyed their company and valued their loyalty. They in turn were anxious to be worthy of him, pleasing to him, useful to him, and responsive to his influence and direction. Friendship, on this basis, would flourish, although never a friendship between equals.

It is commonly observed that by living happily together a husband and wife become increasingly alike, each influencing the other in the way they think and even speak. It is the same for anyone who lives for long with the living God. We start to think along the same lines. We react as he would react; we say the kind of things he would say; we become increasingly like him. This is

---

[1] Isaiah 41:8
[2] Exodus 33:11
[3] Job 29:4
[4] John 15:15

how an ordinary person becomes a godly person. This is how trust grows and eventually becomes unshakable.

A Question of Trust

A relationship between two people will be as strong or as weak as the trust between them. It sometimes happens that a relationship will break down when we cease to have complete trust in one another. Unhappiness will enter a marriage, for example, when a husband loses confidence in his wife, or a wife loses respect for her husband. Mistrust enters the workplace when an employee is suspected of dishonesty or an employer abuses his authority.

As a child of God my deepest desire is to be worthy of his trust. My greatest fear is that I might do something to disappoint him. But I also need to be sure he will be loyal to me, that he genuinely cares about me and is committed to looking after me. My relationship with Yahweh will start to break down if I turn away from him, make independent decisions, exclude him from areas of my life. It may also falter if, for some reason, I lose confidence in him.

At such times I may need help to understand what is happening. There are disappointments in life and not one of us can escape them. Faith may be severely challenged by an unexpected bereavement, by an accident or illness, or by problems that go unresolved or prayers that seem unanswered. At such times it may appear that our Lord has not fulfilled our expectations. So what exactly has gone wrong?

It may be, of course, that our expectations were unjustified or even absurd. We hoped for a gift he never promised or a protection he never guaranteed in this present age. A boy may flap his hands and expect to fly. A holidaymaker may count on sunshine throughout August. An employee may imagine a quick promotion. A cyclist may hope to avoid a flat tyre. We all may wish to get through winter without catching cold. Such fancies are likely to be frustrated. Anyone who supposes there will be no illness, no opposition, no problems to face in this present world will sooner or later become disillusioned.

But if we have a Father who loves us, will he not give us what we ask for? Will he not work everything for good to those who love him? Will he not give us a better deal than people who do not believe in him at all? Such questions are often asked and need an honest answer.

Firstly, we may have some difficulty identifying a good thing when we see it. It is often said that a child does not know what is good for him. Solomon wondered, "Who knows what is good for man?"[1] In fact we may not know what is good for us at all. Our greatest need may not be for the thing we so urgently demand but for wisdom to request something far better, or for love to pray that it may go to someone else, or for insight to accept that before we ask for a blessing we must be more worthy of it. My best spiritual growth may come through unanswered prayer.

Secondly, we can trust our Father to know exactly what is good. The idea we first had in mind may not fit the bigger picture he had planned. It would not have been quite so good as we supposed. In fact it could have been quite disastrous. The more we begin to think like him, the easier it becomes to identify what he would consider good. Through experience we learn to "discern what is the good and acceptable and perfect will of God."[2] And from Jesus we learn the wisdom of praying, "Not my will but yours be done!"[3]

Thirdly, we learn from the seasons of the year to receive good things in their own good time. Some things our Lord has promised for this season of human history and some for the next, some for this present strange chaotic world and some for the age of eternal life that still lies in the future. We should not expect to pick now the fruit that will ripen then.

Often the problem is my impatience. If I do not really trust my Father, I will insist on having my gift immediately for fear of not getting it at all. A little boy who is promised a new bike will be content to wait till Christmas if he knows his parents always keep their word. But if they often change their mind he will want it now, for fear of not getting it at all. In the Bible are many promises that Yahweh has given to his people. Knowing we can trust him, we learn "to be like those who through *faith* and *patience* receive what God has promised."[4]

As we wait for what we want, our Father may have other good things to give us, to teach us, to work into our character, or to do through us for others. Only when that is done will he add the gift so long desired. A little girl who asks to see the elephants at the zoo may enjoy the seals and marmots along the way to the

---

[1] Ecclesiastes 6:12
[2] Romans 12:2
[3] Luke 22:42
[4] Hebrews 6:12

elephants' enclosure, and enjoy them perhaps more than the long-awaited elephant.

Love that Cannot be Shaken

We have seen how an ordinary human being may begin to live with the eternal God, even now in this present world, aware of and responsive to his love. This is a relationship we will value above all others and never wish to lose.

A car with four wheels will come to a halt if just one of its tyres is flat. If a relationship of love breaks down, there has usually been a failure in one of four essential things.

The first of these is loyalty. Jesus was utterly loyal to his disciples and he appreciated their loyalty to him. When they were criticised, he defended them. When they were harassed, he demanded of their persecutor, "Why are you persecuting *me*?"[1] Love requires this intense loyalty. It means that, whatever happens, we are known to be on the same side with the same objectives and concerns. He supports us through thick and thin, and when called upon, we too will stand up and speak for him. No one can possibly doubt we belong to him.

Then secondly, we know from experience that loyalty builds trust. The disciples learned to trust their Lord because they found him worthy of their complete confidence. He could resolve the most baffling problems of life in this world and the next, and he was committed to doing this for them. It was more of a surprise that he was willing to trust them too. Sending them out in his name, he staked his reputation on them. We know enough about our Lord to have complete trust in him, and we want to be worthy of his trust in us.

The third thing is thankfulness. Grateful appreciation adds warmth to any relationship. The Bible writers were thankful people, and with good reason. Every time we count our blessings we grow in our love for the one who sends them. We also have reason, more surprisingly, to believe that our Lord values our efforts too, however inadequate we may think they are. To some he will say, "Well done, good and faithful servant. You have been faithful over a little; I will set you over much."[2] To receive such

---

[1] Acts 26:14
[2] Matthew 25:21

affirmation from the eternal God will be an astonishing delight, if we are indeed found worthy.

Then fourthly, love will do all it can for the happiness of a person who is deeply loved. To upset someone I love would be a grief to us both. To please them will be a pleasure to us both. If I truly love someone, my ambition will be to make them as happy as I can. Their joy is my delight. That is why, living day by day with our Lord, "we make it our aim to please him."[1] And it is wonderful to know that he too takes pleasure in what we do.[2]

Loyalty, trust, thankfulness and a desire to please – these all make for a happy life with the Lord our God. But knowing how every relationship involving human beings is at risk of breaking down, we live in constant danger. The temptations of the world, the tricks of the enemy, the strength of physical desire, the weakness of human resolve – all are at work to undermine and destroy the love that unites us with our Lord. If I am found to be disloyal, mistrusting, unthankful, displeasing, I will see the relationship fall apart.

That is why we are so strongly urged, "Keep yourselves in the love of God."[3] Do not step away from the love he has for you. Do not be found unworthy of his loyalty, his trust, his thankfulness and his pleasure in you. Keep the relationship right and true – always loyal, always trusting, always thankful, always quick to please. That is the Christian's secret of a happy life.

Evidence of Love

Now we meet a man who taught large crowds about the love of God, yet seriously doubted he had ever succeeded in loving God himself.

John Wesley is one of the best-known Christians of all time. In the course of fifty years he rode 250,000 miles on horseback, preaching on average two or three times a day, in every town and village he came to. Throughout his life he lived as cheaply as possible, providing Bibles and helping other preachers, and ended his days as a poor man with only a few coins to his name. Wesley clearly believed his message to be true and vitally important – so important indeed that everyone must hear it, whatever the cost to his comfort or his pocket.

---

[1] 2 Corinthians 5:9
[2] Proverbs 16:7; Colossians 1:10; Hebrews 13:16; 1 John 3:22
[3] Jude 21

Despite this, in his journals and letters, Wesley several times admitted to great difficulty in loving God. It is well known that in May of 1738 his heart was strangely warmed but by October of that year the warmth had evidently faded. He wrote in his diary, "I cannot find in myself the love of God."[i] Again the following January, "I feel this moment I do not love God."[j]

Discouraged with his weakness, Wesley admitted to feeling more love for his friends and for good food than he did for his maker. In this disconcerting spiritual condition he was travelling constantly on horseback by muddy tracks in any weather, often tired and uncomfortable, preaching the gospel and leading thousands to faith in Christ. It astonished him that his work should be so blessed when he himself had no passionate feelings of devotion, no ecstasies in worship, no mystical experiences in prayer.[k]

This might leave us wondering whether John Wesley, for lack of love, was no better than a noisy gong or a clashing cymbal and so, according to scripture, worth nothing.[l]

We have seen how Jesus affirmed the ancient law that we should love the Lord our God with all our heart, soul, mind and strength. There can be no doubt that Wesley with his soul and mind and strength loved God, whatever his heart might seem to lack. The fact is that despite the dramatic power of his preaching he was not a very emotional man. His feelings would never be a true measure of his love, and in time he came to realise this.

The heart, soul, mind and strength represent four facets of human character responsive to the love of God. As human beings we differ greatly from one another. Some are intellectual, others highly sensitive; some are very emotional, others active and energetic.

Having different personalities, we would expect to become aware of God in different ways, and to respond in different ways to that awareness. An energetic person may first love him with the strength of active service, and some time later become convinced in mind, warm in heart and devoted in soul to the Lord his God. A sensitive person will love him with a tender conscience and then afterwards, with mind convinced and heart aroused, commit his strength to the cause of his Lord. An emotional person will love him with exalted joy before exercising his mind or searching his soul or engaging his strength in whatever his Lord calls him to do. An intellectual person will first love him with a clear and convinced mind, and then devote his soul and commit his strength

---

[l] 1 Corinthians 13:1-3

to the service of his Lord before his heart is touched with any deep emotion.

We differ from one another in temperament and will naturally express commitment in different ways. Yet each of us, in time, should come to love the Lord with all our heart and soul, mind and strength. This must be our goal. Only when this is attained will our love for him be complete.

Meanwhile, knowing our limitations we learn to accept each other as we are, growing together in our love for one another and for him.

The Best of Love

We have seen that love takes many forms. Relationships of love can be surprisingly varied in nature. Although I will generally love people who love me, it is possible for me to love a person who refuses to love me, or even a person I dislike. Indeed, Jesus said, "If you love those who love you, what credit is that to you?"[1]

But he went further when he said, "Love your enemies, do good to those who hate you."[2] A person capable of loving those who hate him must have some inner resources of love that do not depend on receiving love in return. Among us are people for whom love has become instinctive, written deeply into their own character. It has become habitual and natural for them to extend a forgiving and a helping hand to the most unlovable and disagreeable of people.

This we might call one-way love, and it happens far more often than we might suppose. A mother will love her baby when the child knows nothing except its own craving for milk. A father will love his son even while the boy is unhelpful and rude. A daughter will love her disabled mother when the old lady is cranky and ungrateful. The love flows in just one direction.

It is even possible to love someone who is unaware of us. You may have a profound and affectionate regard for an actor perhaps, or a politician or a sportsman. You may sign a petition or join a demonstration in support of someone who has never heard of you. You may pay for the education of a child in Africa who does not know your name.

---

[1] Luke 6:32
[2] Luke 6:27

These are all examples of one-way love, and we cannot say it is a bad thing. It is good and right in many circumstances. But it is not the same as two-way love. And in some circumstances it is not right at all. Sadly there are marriages where love is all one way, receiving little or no acknowledgment or response. Rarely can such a marriage survive. Friendships too will fade when communication is all in one direction. I can write a letter to an old school friend, and a second letter, but if he does not reply, the friendship is likely to lapse. Love between two people will probably die if one is active and the other entirely passive. When that happens, love has shrivelled into a duty and an obligation.

We do not want this kind of one-way relationship with Yahweh the Lord our God. If I offer worship and obedience, receiving nothing in return, the love flows just one way. If he provides my daily bread and keeps me from danger, receiving no acknowledgment from me, the love flows just one way. Such love is likely to weaken and fail. We want and need a living relationship with our Father in heaven, a willing exchange of love in which we respond to him and he responds to us. We need to know him and love him as a person like ourselves.

To our delight this is exactly what he has in mind. He enjoys the interaction of a two-way love. He has never been willing for us to go it alone. "He yearns jealously over the spirit that he has made to dwell in us."[1] In past times Yahweh longed for a response from the Israelites. "All day long," he said, "I have held out my hands to a disobedient and contrary people."[2] When we cry out to him he is more than ready to hear us and reply. "Call to me," says the Lord, "and I will answer you."[3]

That is why we pray, knowing he wants to hear, knowing he wants to deal with the concerns we bring to him. From experience David could testify, "Yahweh hears when I call to him."[4] Peter agreed: "The eyes of the Lord are on those who please him, and his ears are open to their prayer."[5]

This indeed is our daily experience. I draw near to him and he draws near to me. I pray for comfort and am comforted. I ask for something to happen and it does. I ask for patience and receive fresh strength. I ask for wisdom and suddenly understand. I pray

---

[1] James 4:5
[2] Romans 10:21
[3] Jeremiah 33:3
[4] Psalm 4:3
[5] 1 Peter 3:12

for guidance and then know the way to go. Whenever I turn to him I have his answer because he loves me.

Then as he speaks to me, he too looks for my response. His Spirit convicts me of some fault and I quickly put it right. He shows me a verse of scripture and I take it to heart. He leads me to someone in need and I am ready to help. These things I do for my Lord because he has won my loyalty and my love. My desire is to be always available, always aware, always responsive to his call. Jesus said, "Whoever accepts my instructions and follows them, he it is who loves me."[1] That is how love works.

---

[1] John 14:21

TO LIVE WITH HIM

10.

His Spirit in Us

When Jesus came to earth he brought the eternal God to us where we are and in ways we can easily comprehend. He simply solved whatever problems there were for the people around him. But he did not stay for long. He died, and when he rose from death – his disciples tell us – he took them to a hill and left them there. They stood gazing after him.

In that moment how would they feel? Disappointed, devastated perhaps, uncertain, abandoned. Once more they were on their own. The infinite Yahweh who had come so close was now as far away as ever.

But Jesus had promised he would not leave them like orphans or street children to fend for themselves in a corrupt and often tragic world. He told them to wait a few days. The eternal God would come once more to earth, not in the form of a man they could see and hear and embrace but closer to them than that. He would come to them as he most naturally is, as an invisible spirit, as a continuous inspiration from within – as electricity moves in a cable or as heat occupies a stone or a cup of tea. "You will receive power," said Jesus, "when the Holy Spirit has come upon you."[1]

There is a great difference between having God all around and having his presence in me. If he is outside of me, I may pray to him and seek to please him while remaining the same person that I

---

[1] Acts 1:8

99

always was. But if he is inside me, I am no longer the same at all. There is a warmth and an energy in me that I could not generate myself. It is the difference between a house depending on street lamps for its brightness and one lit up from within, or between a plank of sawn timber and a tree bearing leaves and fruit. It is the difference between a lorry with a dry and empty tank and one that can transport great loads. The power, in reality, has been turned on.

I no longer think the way I did, or act or speak the way I did, for now I am capable of so much more. His own nature is taking root like a seed in good soil and begins to grow prodigiously, moving me as it moved Jesus to a life of faith, purity, compassion and fearless determination. An ordinary human being is rapidly becoming a man or woman of God.

We accept that the infinite Yahweh is always everywhere. But when Jesus was on earth, Yahweh was especially in him. Now he is especially in me. And he is in all who belong to him – the old gentleman sitting on the park bench (for he too has put his trust in Jesus) and the young mother pushing her baby along the path (for she too belongs to him). They also are filled with the Spirit of God and in touch with him. I will learn to trust them completely for they are godly people. They may be very different from me, and they may have struggles and shortcomings of their own, but as my new spiritual family they share my new life in the Spirit.

There is a great contrast between the old life and the new. Suddenly we understand what is going on. Everything makes sense. "We have received the Spirit sent by God so we may understand the things that God has freely given us."[1] Because "we have the mind of Christ" we begin to see the world and the people in it with fresh eyes.[2] Knowing that "he who began a good work in you will carry it on to completion," we feel a new confidence in ourselves and in others.[3] Fresh reserves of strength and resolution begin to flow: "love, joy, peace, patience, kindness, goodness, faithfulness, gentleness and self-control."[4] These are the fruit of the Spirit, and the more we are filled with the Spirit of our Lord, the more strongly are these energies at work in us.

But then something happens. I react badly to someone, or I do something dishonest, and feel ill at ease. Upsetting and quenching

---

[1] 1 Corinthians 2:12
[2] 1 Corinthians 2:16
[3] Philippians 1:6
[4] Galatians 5:22-23

the Spirit of my Lord in me, I find the flow of spiritual power is choked. Peace of heart gives way to disquiet and uneasiness.

This is certainly worrying, but also very helpful. Just as physical pain shows where something is wrong and needs attention, so spiritual discomfort can do the same. The sense of peace and assurance – or of misgiving and foreboding – may often indicate whether or not I am on the right track.

So we have this good advice: "Let the peace of Christ arbitrate in your hearts."[1] Losing the sense of his peace, I will be wise to put right whatever has gone wrong – whatever it is that grieves the Spirit of my Lord in me. And I may be wise to defer an important decision many days till I have the confirmation of his peace.

In this way the Holy Spirit of God comes to you, and you start to live with him. You do what he would like to do if he were where you are. A person filled with the Spirit of Jesus naturally and gladly lives the loving, joyful, peaceful, patient, disciplined life that Jesus lived.

The Wisdom From Above

If only we could always know the best thing to say and the best course to follow in every situation! We would get things done much more easily and avoid many regrettable mistakes.

It would certainly require great wisdom, and this is the most remarkable thing. Such wisdom is promised to us, and especially when we need it most. "If any of you lacks wisdom, you should ask God, who gives generously to all without reproach, and he will give it to you."[2]

It is through his Spirit moving in our heart and mind that Yahweh gives us his wisdom. In the early church a believer would only be qualified for leadership if he were "full of the Spirit and of wisdom."[3] But this would be the normal experience of all who were inspired by the living God. It was Paul's expectation for every new believer. "From the day we heard about you," he said, "we have not ceased to pray for you all, asking that you may be filled with the knowledge of God's will in all spiritual wisdom and understanding."[4]

---

[1] Colossians 3:15
[2] James 1:5
[3] Acts 6:3
[4] Colossians 1:9

Day by day the wisdom we receive enables us to avoid many problems and to resolve many others. It changes our perspectives and priorities. "The wisdom from above is first pure, then peaceable, gentle, open to reason, full of mercy and good fruits, impartial and sincere. And a harvest of all that pleases God is sown in peace by those who make peace."[1]

To live wisely adds value to every moment of the day, for every moment is put to good use. We each have abilities, time, energy, knowledge and experience that can be either well used or wasted. To be following the Maker's instructions, led by his Spirit, is to make the most of the potential that he gives. If your Lord can trust you with responsibility, he will bring significant people to you, send you on vital missions, show you urgent needs that you can meet, suggest projects you can launch. If, on the other hand, he finds you foolish and unreliable, he will simply set you aside. To be full of the Spirit and wisdom is the normal Christian life and we have every incentive to make sure we live that life to the full.

Long ago Nehemiah was deeply troubled about the ruined condition of Jerusalem. He prayed and asked his Lord what could be done. It was Yahweh who then put an idea into his mind and showed him the way ahead. At first, Nehemiah tells us, "I told no one what my God had put into my mind to do for Jerusalem."[2] He needed more information on the ground before starting to rebuild the city. When the walls were finally complete, he once again asked his Lord for guidance. "Then," he tells us, "my God put it into my mind to assemble the nobles and the officials and the people to be enrolled."[3] Agreement was soon reached for the administration of the city according to the law of Moses. It was Yahweh who revealed the plan – who placed the ideas in Nehemiah's mind – and who gave him the wisdom and patience he then needed in order to accomplish it.

We read of many other occasions in the Bible when the Spirit of God gave wisdom to his people and showed them what to say or where to go. Simeon was moved by the Spirit to enter the temple courts. Stephen's hearers could not resist the wisdom and the Spirit by which he spoke. The Spirit of the Lord took Philip away to Azotus, sent Barnabas and Saul on their mission from Antioch,

---

[1] James 3:17-18
[2] Nehemiah 2:12
[3] Nehemiah 7:5

gave the apostles wisdom to resolve a serious conflict, and guided Paul many times in the course of his missionary journeys.[1]

Still today in every circumstance we can become aware of the best thing to say and do – filled with the Spirit and with wisdom – as the peace of Christ arbitrates in our hearts to confirm the ideas that come to us from the living God.

A Quiet Time

Many people find it helpful to start each day with a quiet time, seeking guidance from the Lord. You might read a chapter or two from the Bible, think about it carefully and then pause. Now is the time to listen with heart and mind, to receive wisdom from above and to understand what his Spirit is saying to your spirit. As you ponder your circumstances, ideas will come to you. You may wish to write them down. This is how someone has described it in their experience:

"The first thoughts may be very different from what you expect. They could be about the kind of task you are meant to take on in the world. Or they might be about something that has been niggling your conscience for a long time. As we compare our lives with Christ's standards of absolute honesty, absolute purity, absolute unselfishness, absolute love, things come to mind that need to be put right. There may be money to pay back. Things we had 'borrowed' to be returned. Apologies to be made for hate or jealousy or for hurts inflicted. Habits to be cut out or a wrong relationship to be ended. The only conditions for getting God's guidance are to be honest about the thoughts that come and to be ready to carry them out.

"God does not tell us where we have been wrong without giving us the power to put things right. There is a force outside ourselves which can root out old habits and faults we supposed would be with us for life. And there is the power of Jesus to forgive and free us from the past and make us new and different people...

"Not every thought that comes in a time of listening is necessarily from God. But we are more likely to hear that

---

[1] See for example Luke 2:27; Matthew 4:1; Acts 6:10; 8:39; 13:2-4; 15:28; 16:6-7; 19:21; 20:22-23.

voice if we take time to listen than if we do not. To make sure that thoughts are not our own selfish wishes, they can be tested by the absolute standards of honesty, purity, unselfishness and love, by Christ's life and by church teaching.

"As we start each day with the question, 'What does God want me to do?', creative thoughts come. A new angle on a problem. Ideas which could lead to far-reaching changes in a person or a situation. A plan for school, home, community and country. Life becomes a thrilling adventure."[1]

Each day brings something new. Then at the end of the day there will be time to reflect: How has it gone? Did I always say the right thing? Did I always do the right thing? What have I learned today? Did I gain fresh insight into my circumstances and the people around me? Am I living as a true Bible Christian? Am I growing more like Jesus – in honesty, purity, unselfishness and love? Am I becoming a person my Lord can entrust with greater responsibility?

If so, the quest for the living God is over and the adventure of living with him has begun.

A Most Interesting Life

Those who do not know us may assume that Christian people are thinking all the time about religious ceremonies and duties. Or they may suppose we particularly like community singing. Or perhaps we feel in need of a little religion on Sundays to make up for the rest of the week. They may imagine that our priority in life is to avoid smoking or swearing or getting drunk. They would be surprised to know there is more to it than that. Many indeed are puzzled to understand why Christians find their faith of such absorbing interest. What is so fascinating about it?

The truth is that living in touch with our creator changes everything. The world and its inhabitants no longer look the same. We see possibilities in everything and everyone. It is simply a question of knowing, at any moment, what we are called to do with those possibilities.

A follower of Jesus is not thinking all the time about religious practice or belief but about every other subject that comes into view as a consequence of belief. Issues of concern to a psychologist or sociologist will certainly concern us too, for we care deeply about the people around us. Politics and economics find a significant place in our unconventional worldview. Geography and history enable us to understand the way things are. Linguistic studies help us communicate the truth. Engineering equips us to improve the quality of life for many in great need. Physics and chemistry, biology, geology and mathematics all help us understand the created world and prepare us to make better use of it. And of course the vast field of medicine opens up as we labour to relieve as much suffering as we can.

A believer is as involved in the world and usually much more involved than his unbelieving friends. He has far more to offer because, unlike them, he does not try to rule its creator out of it. All around us we see so much good gone wrong, and we believe we have the means to put it right. Our awareness that this world has been designed and spoiled, and will one day be restored, gives us a great interest in everything and everyone, and especially in the process and prospect of their restoration. If our maker has assured us that disease, decay and death will soon be gone for ever, we have some wonderful news for this fragile and most anxious planet. To live with Yahweh in his creation and help him solve its problems, while preparing for life in a far better world, becomes a cause so worthwhile and an adventure so stimulating that nothing can remotely equal it.

Along with this comes the assurance that certain unique tasks have been allotted to each one of us, exactly suited to the ability and experience he has given. The Bible says, "God has made us what we are, created anew through Christ Jesus, so we may do the good things he has planned for us to do."[1]

Living with the Lord touches every part of life – every friendship, every choice, every encounter, every decision. It influences how I care for my wife, raise my children, respond to my neighbours, support my workmates, answer the telephone and open my front door. Every day brings fresh needs and opportunities. Going where he leads me to go, and doing what he gives me to do, I see all sorts of things change for the better. Helping others find their way to him, I see distress turn to delight, fear to assurance, anger to forgiveness, despair to hope. Nothing else is half so interesting as this, or half so worthwhile. And working with him, before I know it, I have learned to love him with all my heart, soul, mind and strength.

---

[1] Ephesians 2:10

Is Anyone There?

Every climber, reaching the highest summit of a mountain, will pause to rest and enjoy the view. Our quest for the living God has brought us far, and now we can look back along the path we have followed.

Sincere and honest enquiry has shown us how little we can really know about the infinite eternal *elohim*, but how warmly we may love him, and how wonderfully we may live with him.

At the outset we felt a certain restlessness but also a sense of wonder. In the natural world we saw enough evidence of design to be sure it did not fall into place by accident. In our human abilities and highest ideals we found some clues to the character of the one who made us.

We saw how people in ancient times became aware of an infinite being of great and awesome majesty and learned that his name is Yahweh – the one who always is, everywhere. We watched as Jesus came to show us what he is really like.

In the presence of the divine, men and women would fall to their knees and worship with amazement and keen expectation. Often they knew and understood very little but firmly believed what little they did know. Investigating matters of uncertainty, we found points we could be sure of, building from first principles a statement of definite faith.

After this quest for knowledge, we gave some thought to love. Clearing away the hindrances, we saw how a relationship that starts with a fact may then become a choice and a commitment. But a cold heart we found incapable of love, and a warm heart sometimes wasting love on things quite unworthy.

Seeing how the Bible writers described the love of God, we then considered what a perfect father would be like. With our natural longing for responsive love, we recognised how often we may love someone we do not see. And then, of course, we found that some of us will first respond with heart or soul or mind or strength before love takes over our whole personality.

As children of the living God we have been welcomed into a family inspired by his kindness and compassion. We have so much to look forward to, and especially to a time when every tear will be wiped away and everything on earth will be done with love.

The Bible writers lived in a world as troubled as our own and had no doubt of the power and presence of God to direct and intervene.

The day will come, they said, when wrongs are all put right. In the meantime it is what we achieve against the odds that makes our life heroic.

Wounded perhaps in the battle, we looked back once more to Jesus and his disciples, observing how love kindles love, inspiring loyalty, trust, thankfulness and a desire to please. If all else fails, we found that we may simply follow Jesus. He will, as he promised, bring us to God.

Finally, we turned from loving to living – living with Yahweh day by day, led by his Spirit, inspired by his wisdom and fulfilling his purpose. This is the most exciting and challenging adventure of all. Knowing he has planned for me a better life, I long to become a better person, and to prepare indeed for a much better world.

Questions for Discussion

Chapter

1. What evidence do you think there is for the existence of God?
   How far would you be convinced of his existence...
   ... by a sense of peace or joy?
   ... by a perception of design in the natural world?
   ... by your own highest ideals?
   ... by the character of Jesus?
   ... by the testimony of the Bible writers?

2. How much do we really need to know about anything?
   How do you think we might discover what the Lord God is
   like?
   What may we learn about him...
   ... from creation?
   ... from a direct awareness of him?
   ... from the character and work of Jesus?
   ... from the teaching of Jesus?

3. What causes incompatibility between us and our creator?
   How can the problem of incompatibility be overcome?
   What is faith? How would you explain the difference between,
      "I believe in God" and "I have faith in God"?
   How do you think a person with no faith might come to have
      faith?
   How can I be sure my faith is not mistaken?

4. Is there any reason for us to believe what is written in the
      Bible?
   What does the Bible say about God?
   Which titles, names or other words do you like to use when
      speaking about God?
   What is your understanding of worship?
   How might worship happen for you?

5. How do you think love for God differs from other loves?
   Is there a hindrance to loving God that you have faced and
      overcome?
   Are you ever aware of God's loving presence? How does this
      help you?
   How might Jesus help you know and respond to the love of
      God?

6. What is love?
   What evidence is there that God loves us?
   In what ways do people express love for God?
   How might we learn to love God more?
   How might we help one another to love him more?

7. What English words do we have for love? Which of them
      could describe the love of God?
   What difference will it make to you if you are sure the Lord
      God loves you?
   If the Lord God loves me, does this mean he will answer all my
      prayers?
   Does the idea of God as a father help you at all?
   How do you think God brings out the best in each of us?

8. What do you expect the Lord God to do for you in this present world?

How easy would you like your life to be?

How much are you aware of a battle between good and evil?

Why do you think Yahweh allows so much suffering?

What do you think it will be like to live on the new earth?

9. Heart, soul, mind or strength – which of these was your starting point? How did you first start to love the Lord your God?

How would you expect love to reach and transform the other facets of your character?

How do you think we might "keep ourselves in the love of God"?

How might prayer be an expression of love between God and the people he has created?

10. What does it mean to "live with God" at each stage of your life?

Do you think it is possible always to say and do what is best?

How might you discern each day what the Lord wants you to do?

How has your faith changed your view of the world around you?

As believers, what have we to offer to this fragile and most anxious world?

Endnotes

Bible quotations are based on the Masoretic text of the *Biblia Hebraica Stuttgartensia* (2nd edition 1983) and the *Greek New Testament* (4th edition, UBS 1993). In practice we have usually followed the *English Standard Version*, the *New International Version* or the *Good New Bible*.

---

[a] Horace Bushnell, *Sermons for the New Life* (Schribners, 1904), p.83

[b] Augustine, *Confessions* 1:1

[c] Bill Mills & Craig Parro, *Finishing Well in Life and Ministry* (Leadership Resources International, 1997), p.67

[d] Abraham Joshua Heschel, *God in Search of Man* (Farrar, Strauss and Giroux, 1955, 1976), p.46

[e] Heschel, God in Search of Man, p.46

[f] Heschel, *Man is Not Alone* (Farrar, Strauss and Giroux, 1951, 1976), p.165

[g] Erwin W Lutzer, *Failure the Back Door to Success* (Moody, 1975), p.117

[h] Word definitions are drawn from Leon Morris, *Testaments of Love: A Study of Love in the Bible* (Eerdmans, 1981) and eds. M F Unger & W White, *Vine's Complete Expository Dictionary* (Nelson, 1985).

[i] John Wesley, *Journal*, 14 Oct 1738 (ed. B Waugh and T Mason, *The Works of the Reverend John Wesley AM*, 1835)

[j] John Wesley, *Journal*, 4 Jan 1739

[k] John Wesley, Letter to Charles Wesley, 27 June 1766 (ed. John Telford, *The Letters of John Wesley*, Epworth Press, 1931)

[l] Sydney Cook & Garth Lean, *The Black and White Book* (Blandford, 1972), pp.18-21, quoted by kind permission of Mary Lean and Angela Elliott (copyright holders).